Collateral Damage

Collateral Damage

*The Influence of Political Rhetoric
on the Incorporation of
Second-Generation Americans*

SEAN RICHEY

UNIVERSITY OF MICHIGAN PRESS
ANN ARBOR

Copyright © 2023 by Sean Richey
Some rights reserved

This work is licensed under a Creative Commons Attribution-NonCommercial-NoDerivatives 4.0 International License. *Note to users:* A Creative Commons license is only valid when it is applied by the person or entity that holds rights to the licensed work. Works may contain components (e.g., photographs, illustrations, or quotations) to which the rightsholder in the work cannot apply the license. It is ultimately your responsibility to independently evaluate the copyright status of any work or component part of a work you use, in light of your intended use. To view a copy of this license, visit http://creativecommons.org/licenses/by-nc-nd/4.0/

For questions or permissions, please contact um.press.perms@umich.edu

Published in the United States of America by the
University of Michigan Press
Manufactured in the United States of America
Printed on acid-free paper
First published February 2023

A CIP catalog record for this book is available from the British Library.

Library of Congress Cataloging-in-Publication data has been applied for.

ISBN 978-0-472-07581-2 (hardcover : alk. paper)
ISBN 978-0-472-05581-4 (paper : alk. paper)
ISBN 978-0-472-90313-9 (open access ebook)

DOI: https://doi.org/10.3998/mpub.11691056

The University of Michigan Press's open access publishing program is made possible thanks to additional funding from the University of Michigan Office of the Provost and the generous support of contributing libraries.

Cover illustration courtesy of iStock.com / Filipovico18

For Marina, Ken and Joe

Contents

List of Figures   ix

List of Tables   xiii

Acknowledgments   xv

1. Introduction   1
2. A Theory of Collateral Damage in Political Communication   18
3. Conditions Necessary for Collateral Damage   35
4. Trump Rhetorical Analysis   57
5. Rhetoric and Attitudes toward America   71
6. Rhetoric and Attitudes toward the Republican Party and Donald Trump   93
7. Disaggregating the Attitudes of Second-Generation Americans   117
8. Conclusion   136

Appendix   151

Index   159

Digital materials related to this title can be found on the Fulcrum platform via the following citable URL: https://doi.org/10.3998/mpub.11691056

Figures

1	Number of mentions of *immigration* in US newspaper articles from 1984 to 2018	38
2	Number of mentions of *immigration* and the last name of the Republican Party nominee for president in US newspaper articles in presidential election years, from 1984 to 2018	39
3	Number of mentions of *anti-immigration* and *Republican* in the same US newspaper articles from 1984 to 2018	40
4	Number of joint mentions of *anti-immigration* and *Trump* in US newspaper articles from 1984 to 2018	41
5	Interest in presidential elections for second-generation Americans from the ANES survey, 1952–2020	43
6	Average feeling thermometer ratings for illegal immigrants for non–second-generation and second-generation Americans in the 2016 ANES survey	44
7	Thermometer feelings of second-generation Americans toward Republican presidential nominees, 1968 to 2020	46
8	Angry feelings of second-generation Americans toward Republican presidential nominees, 1980 to 2016	47
9	Fear among second-generation Americans toward Republican presidential nominees, 1980 to 2016	48
10	Histogram of sentiment analysis of Trump immigration tweets comparing Trump with past presidents	65
11	Polling support for Trump in the Republican primary in 2015 and 2016 and the dates of two major anti-immigration speeches	68

x · Figures

12	Treatment effects for patriotism	82
13	Histogram of treatment effects for patriotism	83
14	Treatment effects for American identity	84
15	Histogram of treatment effects for American identity	85
16	Percent of second-generation Americans voting for a Republican for president for 1952 to 2020, divided by before Trump was not on the ballot and when Trump was on the ballot in 2016 and 2020 and by Hispanic or not	95
17	Levels of agreement with Trump's ideas on immigration by second-generation and non-second-generation Americans	97
18	Agreement with the respondent having a linked fate with immigrants by second-generation and non-second-generation Americans	98
19	The level of Republican Party identification after exposure to the treatment conditions	103
20	The level of Republican Party identification after exposure to the treatment conditions for conservative second-generation Americans	104
21	The difference in Trump approval after exposure to experimental stimuli for second-generation Americans	106
22	The difference in Trump approval after exposure to experimental stimuli for conservative second-generation Americans	108
23	Second-generation Americans' opinions on changes in Latinos' situation, separated by parental home country	121
24	Second-generation Americans' opinions on which party has more concern for Latinos, separated by parental home country	122
25	Second-generation Americans voting for Trump, separated by parental home country	123
26	Second-generation Mexican Americans' opinions of the Republican nominee from 1980 to 2016	124
27	Comparison of second-generation Mexican Americans' opinions on building the wall at Mexico's border in 2016 with non-Mexican second-generation Americans	125
28	Second-generation Asian Americans' impression of Trump in 2016, separated by parental home country	127
29	Percentage of second-generation Asian Americans voting for Trump in 2016, separated by parental home country	128

30 Percentage of second-generation Asian Americans identifying with the Republican Party in 2016, separated by parental home country   129
31 Second-generation Americans' opinions on building the wall at Mexico's border in 2016 by border state residency   131

Tables

1	Feeling Thermometer Scores for Illegal Immigrants	45
2	Selected Tweets about Immigration by Donald Trump	60
3	Sentiment Analysis of Trump's Immigration Tweets	63
4	Presidential Speeches Mentioning Immigration or Immigrants	66
5	Ordered Logistic Regression Models of Treatment Effect	85
6	Ordered Probit Regression Models for Hispanic Americans	86
7	Ordered Probit Regression Models for Asian Americans	86
8	Determinants of Patriotism and American Identity in 2012 and 2016	88
9	Effect of Exposure to Trump Rhetoric on Identification with the Republican Party	103
10	Effect of Exposure to Trump Rhetoric for Hispanic Americans on Identification with the Republican Party	105
11	Effect of Exposure to Trump Rhetoric for Asian Americans on Identification with the Republican Party	106
12	Effect of Exposure to Trump Rhetoric on Trump Approval	107
13	Effect of Exposure to Trump Rhetoric on Trump Approval for Conservatives	109
14	Determinants of Republican Presidential Vote and Party Identification, 1952–2020	111
15	Determinants of Voting for Trump in 2020	112
16	Determinants of Voting for Party Identification in 2020	112

17	Determinants of Voting for Trump in 2020 by Second-Generation Americans	113
18	Determinants of Voting for a Republican Presidential Candidate for Second-Generation American Democrats and Republicans, 1952 to 2020	132
A1	Test of Unit Homogeneity	153
A2	Effect of Treatment Conditions	153
A3	Survey Questionnaire	154
A4	Summary Statistics	156
A5	Correlation with Unpatriotic and Dependent Variables	157

Acknowledgments

This research received beneficial comments from participants at various panel sessions, presentations, and colloquiums at the American Political Science Association, the Midwest Political Science Association, Georgia State University Department of Political Science, Doshisha University Department of Media, Journalism and Communications, Gakushuin University Department of Political Science, and Chuo University Faculty of Letters. This research received funding from the Office of the Provost at Georgia State University.

CHAPTER 1

Introduction

What impact does anti-immigration rhetoric have on the children of immigrants? Profound cultural angst exists about immigrant incorporation (Segura 2006). This anxiety is reflected in the anti-immigration rhetoric embedded within our current political discourse. This book provides an overview of how political communication influences the process of incorporation. I show that how elites[1] talk about immigration affects how the children of immigrants feel about the United States and its political parties. These feelings, in turn, greatly influence their desire to incorporate into American political parties and society. I also show that regardless of a speaker's intended outcome, what is said can still have a deleterious effect on incorporation desire, a communicative process that I term *collateral damage*. Although collateral damage is most used in a military setting, this term is broadly defined as an "injury inflicted on something other than an intended target" (Merriam-Webster 2020). I show in this book that anti-immigrant rhetoric from political elites inflicts civic injury[2] on second-generation Americans whether they were the intended target or not. I also show, in chapter 7, how this loss is differentiated by the ethnic subgroups—such as Cuban American or Vietnamese Americans—that have had different experiences with the American party system and thereby have differing party affiliations that alter the impact of this rhetoric.

---

1. I define political elites as prominent former or current politicians, elected officials, or government officials.
2. To be clear, I define civic injury as any impact that creates estrangement from the polity and thereby negatively affects political engagement and democracy more broadly. I show below that harsh anti-immigrant rhetoric does that when read by second-generation Americans.

For immigrants and their children, hostile rhetoric may undermine their incorporation into American society by making the United States seem like a less desirable place to incorporate into. Integration is crucial for ensuring that immigrants and their children can access their rights and fully meet their responsibilities as residents of the country. Understanding the causes and barriers to successfully integrating the large current wave of immigrants into American society is crucial. Tam Cho (1999) shows that if immigrants and their children are socialized into believing that America listens to them and values them, they will have more political efficacy, increasing political participation. The evidence is also clear that integration provides economic benefits to immigrants and their children (e.g., Bratsberg, Ragan, and Nasir 2002). Ramakrishnan and Bloemraad (2008) show that immigrant integration leads to greater civic engagement. Thus, if harsh anti-immigrant rhetoric creates estrangement from the United States for second-generation Americans, it could have a long-term negative impact on political society in America.

In this book, I describe the dominant theoretical debates about immigrant incorporation and outline my collateral damage theory of adverse effects from political communication in the first chapters. I then show why the second generation is the decisive group for incorporation, which justifies my focus on them. I then detail critical recent examples of anti-immigration using President Donald Trump's rhetoric as a test case. In the chapters that follow, I bring new experimental and survey evidence to bear on the question by examining how political communication influences the incorporation process of the children of immigrants. To conduct these analyses, I created several novel surveys with between 500 and 1,000 second-generation Americans, providing this book with more survey data from this understudied group than was previously available.[3]

I focus on the main avenue of political communication that may influence immigrant attitudes toward incorporation: elites' anti-immigration rhetoric. I find that exposure to such speech is off-putting and leads the children of immigrants to be less likely to be patriotic, less likely to embrace an American identity, and express less support for the Republican Party. Thus, this rhetoric significantly impacts incorporation into either America or the Republican Party, whether intentional or not. This outcome shows collateral damage from political communication that adversely affects immigrant incorporation.

More specifically, by drawing on ideas about elite cues and social iden-

---

3. The survey questionnaires are available in the appendix.

tity theory, I posit that anti-immigration rhetoric will be perceived as an attack on a group that members of the second generation identify with because it includes their parents by definition. Attacks against "their" group are thus similar to attacks on themselves and may decrease their allegiance with the larger society. To investigate these effects, in 2016, I conducted an online survey experiment with samples of US citizens with two foreign-born parents matched to nationally representative census data for this group. In 2017, I replicated the survey experiment with online samples of US citizens with two foreign-born parents and two US-born parents, again matched to nationally representative census data for these groups. In 2018, I also conducted surveys on the attitudes and beliefs toward incorporation in general and the US political system with nationally representative data from second-generation Americans. I use these and other data to test the impact of elites' growing use of anti-immigration rhetoric and show how it affects second-generation Americans.

Because Trump typically directs his rhetoric against "illegal immigrants," I used this terminology in the survey experiments' treatments. Although the study participants were US citizens and were not themselves undocumented, I found a clear negative impact from exposure to Trump's hostile rhetoric against undocumented immigrants. These results show that elite anti-immigration rhetoric may have an intergenerational impact that impedes successful integration for the second generation. This finding shows that second-generation Americans perceive elite cues directed against undocumented immigrants as a sign that the United States is less desirable to integrate into. It thus displays the collateral damage of anti-immigration rhetoric from elite persons that may impede integration for the second generation.

I also show how this rhetoric deters second-generation Americans' support for the Republican Party, even among ideologically conservative second-generation Americans who would otherwise be inclined to support it. I show how the second generation's alienation from the Republican Party is crucial for understanding American politics' future, specifically presidential elections within battleground states. Anti-immigration rhetoric strengthens group identity among second-generation Americans, leading them to counter and oppose the Republican Party. By attacking immigrants, the rhetoric triggers an increase in consciousness by focusing attention on immigration and politicizing it. I also find that not all second-generation Americans follow my thesis, specifically Cuban Americans and Vietnamese Americans.

How to incorporate immigrant populations is a crucial issue for advanced industrial nations (Putnam 2007). Immigration potentially offers excellent advantages for the United States (Hirowatari 1998; Smith and Edmonston 1997). Increasing the supply of high- and low-skill workers benefits modern economies, especially as birth rates decline in many advanced democracies (United Nations Population Division 2000). A better understanding of how communication alters opinion can allow policymakers to escape the easy generalizations commonly made about immigrants and incorporation, supporting better decision-making. Gaining knowledge over the impact of communication toward incorporation may allow insights that facilitate better immigration policies. The increasing foreign-born population also presents several challenges for societies in Europe, Asia, and North America. If these effects are known, this knowledge can result in communicative discourse that is more conducive to successful incorporation. Creating positive intergroup relations during a period of increased immigration may have a long-term beneficial impact. Determining the impact of political communication on incorporation will enable an environment conducive to successfully incorporating these new immigrants.

I will now detail how this book contributes to academic debates on immigration incorporation and generally on political communication.

Contribution to Debates on Immigrant Incorporation

This book adds to several long-running academic debates on how the children of immigrants will be incorporated into the broader American society. This question is crucial because research shows that second-generation children often lag in basic citizenship skills, reducing their power and bifurcating society (Portes and Rumbaut 2001). Their incorporation depends on their view of how welcoming the society is and how responsive the system will be to their problems, which will affect their desire to become incorporated.

In the long-running academic debate over how assimilation will unfold in the modern United States, there are two perspectives on possible assimilation pathways. First is a straight-line assimilation model, which mirrors America's past (Alba and Nee 2003). In this model, immigrants slowly adopt more American identity and cultural practices, increasing with each generation. The second perspective is segmented assimilation, which says that some immigrant groups will only assimilate to a certain degree (Portes and Rumbaut 2001). While this debate has unfolded, empirical evidence has been presented that supports both perspectives. Across many objective measures, assimilation does seem to be happening in a straight-line way (see, e.g., Citrin et al. 1997). However, scholars often point to immigrant social movements that are a reaction to anti-immigrant policies and discrimination to show that this new immigration wave is different from what has happened in the past. They argue that this recent wave of immigration will have a more segmented assimilation process.

There is certainly much evidence that immigrants face discrimination (Fetzer 2000; Kinder and Kam 2009). If so, it could be that this intense period of anti-immigration feelings could spark resistance to the traditional straight-line assimilation model. Telzer and Vazquez Garcia (2009), for example, find that Latinas experience a considerable level of discrimination based on skin tone. Beyond America, anti-immigration feelings have grown worldwide (see Richey 2010; Hainmueller and Hiscox 2007). Hopkins (2010) shows that we can expect a pronounced anti-immigrant feelings if a prominent immigration wave is combined with anti-immigrant rhetoric from elites. This finding describes the current American situation well. In response to this discrimination, protest movements—often run by the children of immigrants—that have sparked resistance to assimilation have been widespread (Zepeda-Millán and Wallace 2013).

Additionally, some scholars believe that immigrants do not wish to assimilate. For example, Huntington (2004, 1) says that "the persistent inflow of Hispanic immigrants threatens to divide the United States into two peoples, two cultures, and two languages [because] unlike past immigrant groups, Mexicans and other Latinos have not assimilated into mainstream US culture." This view, however, takes an overly deterministic view of culture, as we know that culture is a continually changing hybrid that is shared between people and not a permanent, unchanging characteristic. Culture may influence behavior passed across multiple generations, but that culture intermingles with other cultures and technological innovation to produce somewhat different outcomes in just a matter of decades. Thus, it is unclear whether current immigrants' existing cultural perspectives will impede the processes of incorporation or even assimilation. Indeed, in the past periods that are now viewed as having straight-line assimilation, anti-immigration critiques over the lack of cultural similarity from immigrants were profound (Archdeacon 1983). Nevertheless, those groups are now viewed as assimilating in a straight line.

All this information taken together suggests that the level of eventual incorporation for the recent large wave of immigrants has yet to be determined. Some forces could accelerate or decelerate the incorporation levels of immigrants into American society. This book aims to show how political communication will be one of the dominant forces that alter these levels, specifically how anti-immigration rhetoric can impact these processes. By bringing empirical evidence to bear on these two competing theoretical perspectives, this book sheds light on which path immigrants are likely to follow and the likely consequences for American politics. Incorporation is, of course, a two-way street: "Whether or not immigration changes the nature and identity of a people is the product of the collective decisions of two sets of actors—both the immigrants and those in the receiving society" (Fraga and Segura 2006, 283). The potential for intergenerational incorporation to affect American politics is profound. Thus, it is vital to determine the influence of anti-immigration rhetoric on incorporation.

For example, suppose the Republican Party alienates the large current wave of second-generation Americans due to Republican politicians' anti-immigration rhetoric. In that case, we can expect a long-term advantage for the Democratic Party with this significant portion of the population. As second-generation Americans are US citizens, it is essential to remember that their children will also be voters. As parents often pass their party identification on to their children, we can expect an intergenerational impact that will influence American politics for decades to come. Moreover, of course, specific subgroups of second-generation Americans, such as Cuban Americans or Vietnamese Americans, may not respond in this manner due to preheld beliefs about the Republican Party and attitudes toward immigration that are divergent from other immigrant groups.[4]

As part of the incorporation process, developing a partisan identification—an attachment to a political party—is crucial for developing ties with the political system. These ties start a bicausal process whereby those who become interested in one of the political parties and then recruited by that party's mobilization efforts become even more active in politics. Mobilization efforts often target people who are at least somewhat inclined toward that party's direction. Negative political communication may impede the development of partisan identification and attachment to the anti-immigrant party. Because second-generation citizens do not have extended family histories tied to parties in the United States, their party identification is often still in flux.

---

4. Additionally, it is essential to note that this book is focused on the impact of anti-immigrant rhetoric from political elites, not anti-immigrant immigration policies. The Democratic Party has pursued policies—such as increased deportations under President Joe Biden—that some second-generation Americans may view as anti-immigration.

I find that while many second-generation Americans are politically conservative, very few are anti-immigration. Anti-immigration rhetoric may alienate these potential supporters of the Republican Party. Since they make up a growing percentage in many battleground states, such as Florida, Arizona, and Nevada, they may have a disproportionate impact on American politics if they are pushed away from the Republican Party by this hostile rhetoric. Thus, due to its importance to the future of American politics, researching the impact of anti-immigration rhetoric on immigrants and their descendants' attitudes toward party attachment is necessary.

The academic literature on immigration assumes that globalized societies are heading in a multicultural direction (Berry 2001). It assumes, or perhaps even makes the prescription, that host countries need to see themselves as pluralistic societies and thus support ethnic groups remaining distinct elements within society (see Taguchi 1983). Generally, academics push for countries to realize their diversity and to embrace it. What is mainly ignored in the current academic discourse, however, is the desires of immigrants. Do immigrants want to be a separate category, or do they want to incorporate? If so, how much? These are crucial questions, and they require more research on the opinions of immigrants.

The existing evidence is not conclusive. Data from various surveys conducted with immigrants show some want to incorporate (see, for example, Farkas, Duffett, and Johnson 2003). Furthermore, we know from sociological studies that many immigrants quickly incorporate, if they are allowed to (Waters and Jimenez 2005), in such ways as learning the dominant language and embracing the receiving country's culture. In the United States, incorporation is common within two generations, especially for Americans of Mexican descent (Waters and Jimenez 2005).

We do not know how this process is affected by the recent increase in anti-immigration rhetoric from elites. The election of Donald Trump as president of the United States makes this topic particularly important to study. I show in chapter 4 that he often uses harsh anti-immigration rhetoric, which is thoroughly covered by mass media and therefore often heard by second-generation Americans. Thus, while incorporation is typical for immigrants, the impact of contact with the increasingly hostile anti-immigrant discourse is an essential issue to research. Consequently, understanding and addressing the barriers to successful integration are also critical.

Now I examine how current research on political communication is not focused on the unintended effects of communication and show how this book adds to political communication research more broadly.

Contribution to Debates on Political Communication

Scant academic research has been done on how elite rhetoric alters the process of immigrant integration. Even less research examines how the unintended impact of communication can still affect public opinion. Since Trump's messaging is probably not explicitly intended to impede the incorporation of second-generation Americans, any effect in that regard is an unintended by-product of the original communication. Most research assumes that communication is directed at a target with the aim of persuasion, such as the traditional sender-medium-receiver paradigm discussed in chapter 2. Indeed, Trump's rhetoric is intended for a specific targeted audience to persuade them to vote for him and be against illegal immigration. However, in addition to this intended audience, others in society hear his rhetoric, and any impact on these nontargeted receivers has not been studied.

Despite considerable research on elite discourse and racial minorities (see, e.g., White 2007), there has been less work on the impact of such discourse on immigrants or their children. However, Valentino, Brader, and Jardina (2013) show how newspaper coverage focused white opinions about immigration on Latinos, which shows that elite attention can alter perceptions about immigration. Their research and others are focused on the impact of intended communication and ignore any possible unintended effects. This book's chief contribution to political communication research shows how unintended audiences are affected by political communication. Examining unintended audiences opens up a broad new avenue for research. Political communication researchers can investigate how communication affects countless audiences that are not the communicator's original target.

Why Write a Book on the Impact of Trump's Anti-Immigration Rhetoric?

The reason this book is necessary is the significant increase in anti-immigration rhetoric by elites (see chapter 4 for empirical evidence on Trump's rhetoric). This book empirically tests the normative and empirical assumptions implicit in prior work using experimental research and nationally representative survey data to focus on the fallout from harsh rhetoric about immigration. This book is different from prior works because it focuses on elite communication that alienates and marginalizes immigrants' children. I focus on how communication impacts the desire to incorporate into the larger American political society. For example, scholars often focus on elite rhetorical depictions of American identity, but not how elite rhetoric impacts immigrants' attitudes. As such, this book adds to the literature in important and novel ways. I term this impact *collateral damage* because although it may not have been intended to undermine integration, it could affect second-generation Americans' attitudes and create negative reciprocal attitudes toward the United States. Note that this loss occurs for both second-generation Americans and the nation, which loses benefits due to decreased participation in American political life and causes a macro effect on US representational democracy.

Since Trump lost the 2020 election, it may be helpful to address why Trump's rhetoric is featured so prominently in this book. This book studies anti-immigration rhetoric from elites and uses Trump as an example, but it is not specifically a book about Trump. Trump is just one of many politicians who uses intense anti-immigration rhetoric. Many other politicians, such as Tom Cotton from Arkansas, Kris Kobach from Kansas, and Steve King from Iowa, use similar rhetoric. Due to his prominence and importance in American politics, Trump's rhetoric is a practical way to operationalize elite anti-immigration rhetoric.

Simply put, the book is not about Trump. Instead, it is about how anti-immigration elite rhetoric affects those in the second generation, and it happens to use Trump's communication as an exemplar of this type of rhetoric. More importantly, it offers a formal theory that is grounded in decades of communication science that shows that although we typically expect a minimal effect from communication, the conditions are in place for second-generation Americans to potentially be influenced by elite rhetoric such as Trump's due to their lack of socialization into the American political system.

Additionally, it is essential to understand Trump's impact because he may have a multigenerational influence due to the profound coverage of his rhetoric, even though he was only a one-term president. Almost everyone in the second generation will have heard his rhetoric on Mexican immigrants being rapists and killers and so forth. We need to understand what these Americans feel about a country that has nominated and elected a president like Trump. Moreover, since many other politicians may be influenced by Trump's success in the future to take a similar approach to develop a following based on harsh anti-immigration rhetoric, it is crucial to understand how this rhetoric will subsequently influence incorporation processes. After his presidency, he also has an enormous email list of millions that receive daily blasts, often containing anti-immigrant rhetoric. He is potentially running again for president in 2024. Thus, even though Trump was only a one-term president, his influence may alter politics for many years to come. For these reasons, it is important to study Trump specifically and more generally examine how elite rhetoric impacts incorporation processes.

Currently, the issue of immigration is framed by elite rhetoric from two chief sources.[5] The first source of cues for the public are delivered directly from the politicians who bash immigrants. Attacking weak minorities is a standard tool for a specific subset of politicians to get easy name recognition and create interest in their campaigns. President Trump and former Colorado representative Tom Tancredo are perhaps the best-known examples, but dozens of prominent politicians have attacked immigration (Burgess 2004). Patrick Buchanan had a long career that featured many anti-immigrant diatribes. For example, Buchanan (2007) said, "Where the Italians wanted to be part of our family, millions of Mexicans are determined to retain their language and loyalty to Mexico. They prefer to remain outsiders. They do not wish to assimilate, and the nation no longer demands that they do so" (Buchanan 2007, 27). These politicians directly create hostility toward immigration and doubts that it benefits the host country.

The second source of cues is mass media that deliver these messages when they report on anti-immigration rhetoric. It is well established that the media are particularly interested in crime stories due to their ability to spark interest and increase ratings or sales (Barrile 1984). Immigrant crime has been sensationalized by the press, with stories about immigrants' crimes far outnumbering stories on the positive impacts of immigrants (Jacobs, Hooghe, and Vroome 2017). Positive stories are less dramatic than crime stories, so the media focuses on rare examples of murder or rape by immigrants. For the average person, this media coverage frames immigration as a crime issue and inherently harmful (Vincenzo 2019). As part of this media coverage, the new intense anti-immigration rhetoric from prominent politicians, such as a president or presidential nominee,

---

5. For natives, prior research on immigration attitudes has determined that six main factors influence public opinion toward immigration. These six attributes are (1) ideology (McClosky 1964); (2) identification with anti-immigrant political parties (Weldon 2006); (3) economic threat (Burns and Gimpel 2000); (4) demographic attributes (Mayda 2006; Binder, Polinard, and Wrinkle 1997); (5) authoritarianism and tolerance (Altemeyer 1998; Pratto and Lemieux 2001); and (6) diverse social networks (Abrams and Hogg 1998).

will increase the amount of news coverage that has negative frames about immigration. We need to understand what impact these frames have on second-generation Americans and their perceptions of America broadly and the Republican Party specifically.

I now detail each chapter to explain its specific contribution.

Detailed Chapter Outline

Generally, this book is designed to test the determinants of immigrant incorporation for a thriving democratic society. The specific chapters are about support for and barriers to immigrant incorporation based on political communication, such as anti-immigration rhetoric from politicians. Below is an annotated table of contents for the rest of the book.

Chapter 2: A theory of collateral damage. This chapter explicates a novel theory on how presidential rhetoric can have nonminimal effects on unintended audiences. To investigate the potential for political communication to have unintended consequences, I examine communication theory and state specific lemmas from which my theory can be tested. I show how the rhetoric of President Trump and immigration incorporation are highly relevant test cases for this theory. My collateral damage theory is based on decades of research on conditioning and the impact of communication. Simply put, my theory is that highly interested subpopulations who lack political socialization will be differentially influenced by elite rhetoric compared with the uninterested mass public, which has a high degree of political socialization, whether or not they were the intended recipient of the communication. I also theorize that this effect is differentiated by long-term partisan attachment from different ethnic subgroups.

Chapter 3: Conditions necessary for collateral damage. In this chapter, I test the four lemmas described in chapter 2 that are conditions necessary for the theory of collateral damage to be empirically valid, and I provide empirical support for each. Specifically, I show that the media covered Trump's anti-immigration rhetoric so well that most second-generation Americans were fully exposed to it (lemma 1). Also, I show that children of immigrants are attuned to anti-immigration rhetoric because they care about immigrants (lemma 2). I also demonstrate that immigrants' children can be influenced on these topics because they are not highly socialized into beliefs about the United States or its party system (lemma 3). Finally, I provide evidence that the effect is not dependent on Trump's intention (lemma 4). The support for these lemmas leads to being able to test the main theory with the experiments and survey data analysis in the flowing chapters.

Chapter 4: Trump rhetorical analysis. I show in this chapter that there has never been a presidential candidate or president like Trump in terms of rhetoric on immigration. Using content analysis of newspapers, I show how media coverage of Trump's rhetoric is uniquely focused on immigration. Using data on presidential speeches about immigration, I show that Trump focuses on immigration more than any prior president in his speeches. Using quantitative text analysis, I show that his tweets about immigration are empirically and objectively negative. All evidence clearly and unequivocally shows that Trump is different and focused more negatively on immigration than other presidents. It underscores the need for empirical research demonstrating how this different rhetoric affects those who care about this issue, such as immigrants' children. Although many citizens may intuitively believe this, empirically establishing the difference is a necessity. American politics has featured anti-immigration rhetoric since its founding, but since 2015 it was the primary issue in a way that it was never before. This harsh rhetoric is the impetus for my research because we have never had such an intense focus on immigration's negative aspects. This evidence leads to the need to test the impact of this harsh rhetoric in chapters 5, 6, and 7.

Chapter 5: Rhetoric and attitudes toward America. This chapter examines how anti-immigration rhetoric affects second-generation Americans' feelings of American identity and patriotism as a proxy for general incorporation into America. Using Trump's rhetoric as a test case, I conducted a survey experiment with an online sample of US citizens with two foreign-born parents matched to nationally representative US census data. I found that exposure to Trump's anti-immigration rhetoric reduced expressed patriotism and feelings of American identity. I augment these experimental results with national representative survey data that show similar correlations. These results show that elite anti-immigration rhetoric may impede the successful integration for the second generation.

Chapter 6: Rhetoric and attitudes toward the Republican Party and Donald Trump. This chapter extends the findings of chapter 5 by examining how anti-immigration rhetoric affects second-generation Americans' attitudes toward the Republican Party and President Trump. Because second-generation Americans can vote as US citizens and are often clustered in presidential battleground states such as Arizona, their massive size will likely determine many electoral contests. For example, in some states, 20% of the population are immigrants, but presidential elections have been often decided by less than 2% of the population in several of the last five presidential elections. Using a survey experiment from 2017, I find that anti-immigration rhetoric's effects translate into an increased dislike for the Republican Party and Trump among this growing group of young voters. This is even true for ideologically conservative second-generation Americans' attitudes toward Trump. This finding suggests that the long-term impact of Trumpism may be detrimental to the Republican Party. Of course, since dislike for Trump and the Republican Party translates into voting behavior because voters may not like the candidate for the party, I test voting behavior specifically using survey data from 2020 and find lower voting for Trump from second-generation Americans while controlling for other possible determinants, such as socioeconomic status and ideology.

Chapter 7: Disaggregating the attitudes of second-generation Americans. In this chapter, I disaggregate the findings of chapters 5 and 6 to ethnic subgroups of second-generation Americans. Using three new datasets collected during the 2016 election or afterward, I analyze important subgroups within Latinos and Asian Americans. Two of these three datasets specifically target large samples of the subethnic groups within the more prominent pan-ethnic labels. Using hypotheses derived from the theory stated in chapter 2, I posit that Mexican Americans will be more resistant to Trump. I also hypothesize that Cuban Americans and Vietnamese Americans will not be as resistant to Trump due to their long-standing party identification with the Republican Party. Ronald Reagan established with Cuban Americans and Vietnamese Americans that the Republican Party was on their side because of his clear anticommunism and tough stances with the Castro regime and the Communist Party of Vietnam. Using the literature on motivated reasoning as a theoretical guidepost, I suggest that these Republican-leaning subgroups may disproportionately view negative information about the Republican Party and President Donald Trump as cognitively dissonant to what they previously believed.

The data clearly shows that the hypotheses are validated. For example, when analyzing second-generation Mexican Americans, Dominican Americans, Salvadoran Americans, Spanish Americans, and other Latinos, I find that Mexican Americans are most likely to be against Trump's build-the-wall idea. I also find that Cuban Americans are the most likely to think that the Republican Party cares more about Latinos during Trump's presidency. Cuban Americans are also the only group that thinks that the situation for Latinos has improved during the Trump presidency. All other subgroups of Latinos think that the situation for Latinos has gotten worse during the Trump presidency.

The data for Asian Americans allowed me to analyze opinions about Trump by Bangladeshi, Cambodian, Chinese, Filipino, Hmong, Indian, Japanese, Korean, Pakistani, and Vietnamese second-generation Americans. Like what was found for Cuban Americans, I find that Vietnamese Americans are by far the most likely to support the Trump presidency, have a favorable impression of Trump, and remain loyal to the Republican Party. I also analyze disaggregating second-generation Americans by examining how political geography influences support for Trump's ideas and the influence of party identification on voting for Trump in 2020.

Chapter 8: Conclusion. I conclude the book by summarizing the arguments and results. In this chapter, I provide a brief overview of the findings and speculate on the future of immigrant incorporation. I then suggest seven ways future researchers could successfully analyze political communication and immigrant incorporation in conjunction. Also, I list and examine other potential forces that may delimit political incorporation.

Additionally, the appendix has many regression models and data analysis that are referenced in the text or are underlying or used to create graphs or other features in the book.

References

Abrams, Dominic, and Michael A. Hogg. 1998. "Prospects for Research in Group Processes and Intergroup Relations." *Group Processes and Intergroup Relations* 1:7–20.

Alba, Richard, and Victor Nee. 2003. *Remaking the American Mainstream: Assimilation and Contemporary Immigration.* Cambridge, MA: Harvard University Press.

Altemeyer, Robert. 1998. "The Other Authoritarian Personality." In *Advances in Experimental Social Psychology*, edited by Mark P. Zanna, 47–92. San Diego: Academic Press.

Archdeacon, Thomas J. 1983. *Becoming American: An Ethnic History.* New York: Free Press.

Barrile, Leo. 1984. "Television and Attitudes about Crime: Do Heavy Viewers Distort Criminality and Support Retributive Justice?" In *Justice and the Media: Issues and Research*, edited by Ray Surette, 141–58. Springfield, IL: Charles C. Thomas.

Berry, John W. 2001. "A Psychology of Immigration." *Journal of Social Issues* 57 (3): 615–31.

Binder, Norman E., J. L. Polinard, and Robert D. Wrinkle. 1997. "Mexican American and Anglo Attitudes toward Immigration Reform: A View from the Border." *Social Science Quarterly* 78:324–37.

Bratsberg, B., J. F. Ragan, and Z. M. Nasir. 2002. "The Effect of Naturalization on Wage Growth: A Panel Study of Young Male Immigrants." *Journal of Labour Economics* 20 (3): 568–79.

Buchanan, Patrick J. 2007. *State of Emergency: The Third World Invasion and Conquest of America*. New York: St. Martin's Press.

Burgess, Chris. 2004. "Maintaining Identities: Discourses of Homogeneity in a Rapidly Globalizing Japan." *Asian Studies Review* 28:223–42.

Burns, Peter, and James G. Gimpel. 2000. "Economic Security, Prejudicial Stereotypes, and Public Opinion on Immigration Policy." *Political Science Quarterly* 115:201–25.

Citrin, Jack, Donald P. Green, Christopher Muste, and Cara Wong. 1997. "Public Opinion toward Immigration Reform: The Role of Economic Motivations." *Journal of Politics* 59 (3): 858–81.

Farkas, Steve, Ann Duffett, and Jean Johnson. 2003. *Now That I'm Here: What America's Immigrants Have to Say about Life in the US Today*. Public Agenda Foundation. Accessed September 19, 2007. https://files.eric.ed.gov/fulltext/ED473894.pdf

Fetzer, Joel S. 2000. *Public Attitudes toward Immigration in the United States, France, and Germany*. New York: Cambridge University Press.

Fraga, Luis R., and Gary M. Segura. 2006. "Culture Clash? Contesting Notions of American Identity and the Effects of Latin American Immigration." *Perspectives on Politics* 4 (2): 279–87.

Hainmueller, Jens, and Michael J. Hiscox. 2007. "Educated Preferences: Explaining Attitudes toward Immigration in Europe." *International Organization* 61 (2): 399–442.

Hainmueller, Jens, and Daniel J. Hopkins. 2014. "Public Attitudes toward Immigration." *Annual Review of Political Science* 17 (1): 225–49.

Hirowatari, Seigo. 1998. "Foreign Workers and Immigration Policy." In *The Political Economy of Japanese Society*, edited Junji Banno, 81–106. Oxford: Oxford University Press.

Hopkins, Daniel J. 2010. "Politicized Places: Explaining Where and When Immigrants Provoke Local Opposition." *American Political Science Review* 104:40–60.

Huntington, Samuel P. 2004. "The Hispanic Challenge." *Foreign Policy* (March–April): 30–45.

Jacobs, Laura, Marc Hooghe, and Thomas de Vroome. 2017. "Television and Anti-immigrant Sentiments: The Mediating Role of Fear of Crime and Perceived Ethnic Diversity." *European Societies* 19 (3): 243–67.

Kinder, Donald R., and Cindy D. Kam. 2009. *Us against Them: Ethnocentric Foundations of American Opinion*. Chicago: University of Chicago Press.

Mayda, Anna Maria. 2006. "Who Is against Immigration? A Cross-Country Investigation of Individual Attitudes toward Immigrants." *Review of Economics and Statistics* 3:510–30.

McClosky, Herbert. 1964. "Consensus and Ideology in American Politics." *American Political Science Review* 58 (2): 361–82.

Merriam-Webster.com Dictionary, s.v. "collateral damage," accessed February 20, 2020, https://www.merriam-webster.com/dictionary/collateral%20damage

Portes, Alejandro, and Ruben G. Rumbaut. 2001. *Legacies: The Story of the Immigrant Second Generation*. Berkeley: University of California Press.
Pratto, Felicia, and Anthony F. Lemieux. 2001. "The Psychological Ambiguity of Immigration and Its Implications for Promoting Immigration Policy." *Journal of Social Issues* 57 (3): 413–30.
Putnam, Robert D. 2007. "*E Pluribus Unum*: Diversity and Community in the Twenty-First Century; The 2006 Johan Skytte Prize Lecture." *Scandinavian Political Studies* 30 (2): 137–74.
Ramakrishnan, S. Karthick, and Irene Bloemraad. 2008. "Making Organizations Count: Case Studies in California." In *Civic Hopes and Political Realities: Immigrants, Community Organizations, and Political Engagement*, edited by S. Karthick Ramakrishnan and Irene Bloemraad, 45–76. New York: Russell Sage Foundation.
Richey, Sean. 2010. "The Impact of Anti-Assimilationist Beliefs on Attitudes towards Immigration." *International Studies Quarterly* 54 (1): 197–212.
Schildkraut, Deborah J. 2005. *Press One for English: Language Policy, Public Opinion, and American Identity*. Princeton: Princeton University Press.
Segura, Gary M. 2006. "Symposium Introduction: Immigration and National Identity." *Perspectives on Politics* 4 (2): 277–78.
Smith, James P., and Barry Edmonston, eds. 1997. *The New Americans: Economic, Demographic, and Fiscal Effects of Immigration*. Washington, DC: National Academy Press.
Taguchi, Sumikazu. 1983. "A Note on Current Research of Immigrant Groups in Japan." *International Migration Review* 17 (4): 699–714.
Tam Cho, Wendy K. 1999. "Naturalization, Socialization, Participation: Immigrants and (Non)Voting." *Journal of Politics* 61 (4): 1140–55.
Telzer, Eva H., and Heidie A. Vazquez Garcia. 2009. "Skin Color and Self-Perceptions of Immigrant and U.S.-Born Latinas: The Moderating Role of Racial Socialization and Ethnic Identity." *Hispanic Journal of Behavioral Sciences* 31 (3): 357–74.
United Nations Population Division. 2000. *Replacement Migration: Is It a Solution to Declining and Ageing Populations?* New York: United Nations.
Valentino, Nicholas A., Ted Brader, and Ashley E. Jardina. 2013. "Immigration Opposition among U.S. Whites: General Ethnocentrism or Media Priming of Attitudes about Latinos?" *Political Psychology* (2): 149–66.
Vincenzo, Memoli. 2019. "Media Use, Political Efficacy and Anti-immigrant Feelings in Host Countries." *Contemporary Italian Politics* 11 (4): 415–28.
Waters, Mary C., and Tomas Jimenez. 2005. "Assessing Immigrant Assimilation: New Empirical and Theoretical Challenges." *Annual Review of Sociology* 31 (1): 105–25.
Weldon, Steven A. 2006. "The Institutional Context of Tolerance for Ethnic Minorities: A Comparative, Multilevel Analysis of Western Europe." *American Journal of Political Science* 50 (2): 331–49.

White, Ismail K. 2007. "When Race Matters and When It Doesn't: Racial Group Differences in Response to Racial Cues." *American Political Science Review* 101 (2): 339–54.

Zepeda-Millán, Chris, and Sophia J. Wallace. 2013. "Racialization in Times of Contention: How Social Movements Influence Latino Racial Identity." *Politics, Groups and Identities* 1 (4): 510–27.

CHAPTER 2

A Theory of Collateral Damage in Political Communication

This chapter explicates a novel collateral damage theory of political communication on how presidential rhetoric can have nonminimal effects on unintended audiences. To investigate the potential for political communication to have such consequences, I examine communication theory and state specific lemmas that build toward my theory. I show how the rhetoric of President Trump and immigrant incorporation creates a highly relevant test case for my theory. My theory draws on decades of research on conditioning and the impact of communication. Simply put, it posits that elite rhetoric will be more likely to alienate highly interested subpopulations who lack political socialization, compared with the uninterested mass public, which has a higher degree of political socialization, regardless of whether the communication was intended for the subpopulations. I also posit that not all children of immigrants follow my thesis, specifically Cuban Americans, Vietnamese Americans, and Mexican Americans due to unique factors that differentially influence these groups.

I fully explicate my collateral damage theory with a formal model in this chapter, using some basic lemmas that are necessary for it to be verified (discussed in-depth and tested in chapter 4):

1. The elite rhetoric will be broadcast widely so that subpopulations will be exposed to it.
2. These subpopulations are disproportionately interested in the topic of the rhetoric.

3. These subpopulations do not have a sizeable prior set of beliefs and opinions on the rhetorical topic.
4. The impact of the elite rhetoric does not depend on whether it was intended to cause harm to the subpopulation or not.

My theory is partially grounded in prior research on communication effects, which forms a well-established literature extending over almost a century. Scholars have debated the effect of mass media on the public since the famous John Dewey–Walter Lippmann debates in the early 1920s on propaganda on public opinion (Whipple 2005). These debates focused on many of the important fundamental questions that we currently ask about democratic politics, such as whether a sophisticated citizenry is feasible. As such, a study of the possible impact of Trump's rhetoric fits into an academic debate with a long pedigree and voluminous literature, which I now briefly summarize to lead to a formal statement of my theory.

The literature on communication effects is vast, and this subject has been explored through almost every methodology for decades. My overview here presents the developments in communication science in essentially chronological order, and I consider the findings in light of their potential relevance for media effects. I start with the early information theories of communication, representing the antecedents to the minimal effects paradigm of political communication.

The Minimal Effects Paradigm

Generally speaking, there have been two main paradigms in communication science. The first dominant paradigm was minimal effects.[1] Although the media is often assumed to influence public opinion profoundly, the classic scholarship on this issue indicates a much more subtle effect (see Bennett and Iyengar [2008] for a review).

Early work by the Columbia school scholars showed that mass media had minimal effect on public opinion because most people did not change their vote choice, even after exposure to months of campaign communication (Lazarsfeld, Berelson, and Gaudet 1944). They found that political communication's main effect during a campaign was to alert the public to an upcoming election and remind them of their connections to the parties

---

1. Although, see Simonson (2014) for a critical history on the degree of centrality of this paradigm in communication research.

in the election and the candidates' basic ideological orientations (Berelson, Lazarsfeld, and McPhee 1954). In other words, hearing a speech about an upcoming election did not influence very many people, and the size of that influence was not significant if it registered at all. These early pioneering studies set the stage for the minimal effects paradigm.

According to these studies, the only way mass media persuades is through influencing opinion leaders, who then influence individuals who listen to them through interpersonal communication (Katz 1957). In other words, the media is only effective through a two-step process that requires influencing the people that others listen to. These opinion leaders are influencers because of their expertise in politics—or at least the people in their network view them as experts. However, the influence of opinion leaders is not absolute, nor does it reach everyone. Since media has insignificant direct effects, the two-step flow of communication dilutes the media's influence, leading to a minimal effect on public opinion.

Klapper (1960) further posited that selective exposure allows people who are not interested in politics to tune out objectionable messages. Someone aligned with certain political ideologies can tune into agreeable speakers and ignore those they disagree with. Thus, Klapper argued that minimal effects are also likely because if people do not enjoy what is being said, they simply ignore it.

A central reason for minimal effects is that most people have heard millions of words about politics before interacting with any additional political messaging, such as a campaign commercial or a post on social media, as adults. The average adult hears over 8,000,000 words in a year and has heard over a hundred million of words before reaching adulthood (Logan et al. 2019). Consequently, a 30-second campaign commercial—which may contain at most 100 words—is unlikely to have a profound long-term impact on beliefs or behaviors. Even Trump's largest tweetstorm, about the Mueller report, was only about 200 words in sum, with any specific tweet being less than 20 words due to the 280-character limit of Twitter.

In the years following the early work in the field, scholars established alternative routes for media influence, such as agenda-setting, priming, framing, and so on (see, e.g., Iyengar and Kinder 1987). These alternative avenues do not confirm a direct "hypodermic needle" effect that many people assume rhetoric has over public opinion. Instead, these avenues expand on the indirect ways communication can be effective. For example, presidents can influence the public, particularly when they desire a reaction to public policy opinions (Canes-Wrone 2005). Presidents mold the public into their desired audience by focusing their attention on the issues they want to talk about (Campbell and Jamieson 1990). When "going public," a president can center public consciousness on the issues he wants to highlight (Tulis 1987). Scacco and Coe (2016) posit that in the constant current barrage of 24/7 media—which includes tweets from Donald Trump from early in the morning to very late at night—we have a communication environment best described as the ubiquitous presidency. The sheer amount of content and coverage of presidential communication is suggestive that an influence from rhetoric can be found on what topics are debated in our national discourse. When a president is singularly focused on an issue, continually bringing it up in highly salient and even contentious ways, attention will be drawn to that issue. Trump's rhetoric brought immigration policy to the forefront of American politics. Immigration has been a salient issue since at least the first attempt at comprehensive immigration reform in 2006, but it was not the preeminent issue in the 2008 and 2012 presidential elections as it became in the 2016 election.

Additionally, the literature on priming suggests that once a president is associated with a topic in media coverage, the subsequent analysis and evaluations of their performance become entangled with that issue (Iyengar, Peters, and Kinder 1982). Trump's focus on immigration created a situation in which Americans' evaluations of him were based in part on how well he stopped undocumented immigration.

Edwards (2003), however, shows that on most issues, the supposed impact from the bully pulpit can be overestimated owing to factors highly related to the minimal effects paradigm. Modern presidents cannot persuade the public all the time (Druckman and Holmes 2004; Tedin, Rottinghaus, and Rodgers 2010). While the bully pulpit of the presidency often allows the president to set the agenda in the mass media, notice that this is not a refutation of minimal effects from presidential political rhetoric. By focusing attention on undocumented immigration, and highlighting salacious crimes committed by immigrants, Trump certainly could get Americans to think about immigration when they think about politics. However, this does not mean Americans will agree with or support the ideas he discusses. They may think about his topic—agenda setting—but not be persuaded by what he says about it—minimal effects.

In sum, the basic model of how Trump could negatively affect second-generation Americans' attitudes toward the United States and the Republican Party would not be supported by the minimal effects paradigm. This literature up to this point would suggest minimal effects from Trump's rhetoric on second-generation Americans. Importantly, it is also unclear how agenda setting and priming in Trump's focus on immigration will impact second-generation Americans, who are rarely mentioned in Trump's rhetoric. I, however, explicate a theory below as to why I believe there will be nonminimal effects for this subpopulation. To explore how Trump could be effective, I turn from media studies and examine relevant literature in psychology, particularly on conditioning, to develop a formal model for testing my hypotheses.

Conditional Effects

An extensive debate has developed over the actual efficacy of presidential rhetoric. Some scholars suggest that it has a minimal direct effect on public opinion (e.g., Edwards 2003), while others argue that its success depends on contingent factors in the political environment, such as popularity, polarization, timing, and so forth (Tedin, Rottinghaus, and Rodgers 2010). The latter group emphasizes that presidential rhetoric is influential when the conditions allow it to be (Cohen 2008, 2010; Eshbaugh-Soha 2008; Eshbaugh-Soha and Peake 2011; Eshbaugh-Soha and Rottinghaus 2013). This perspective is essential for my theory because it is conditional on the audience being attentive and not having a high degree of prior political socialization on the rhetoric topics. This type of impact is called conditional media effects. There is also a long literature examining conditional media effects, which became the second dominant paradigm in communication studies. The development of conditional media effects begins with the conditioning literature in psychology, which I now discuss, leading to a formal statement of my theory below.

Contemporaneous with the early communication studies, but not necessarily in collaboration with those scholars, research was being conducted in psychology on how influence occurs (Whorf 1940). This research necessarily included the study of communication because influence is almost always attempted through communicative acts. As such, psychologists quickly began studying the effects of communication. Initially, these effects were termed under the phrasing of "conditioning," whereby some communicative action would lead to a response. Later, understanding the relationships became more sophisticated; however, this research's foundations are essential in developing my collateral damage theory. I now outline one of the most prominent early models of influence in communication, the Shannon and Weaver Model.

Shannon and Weaver Model

Since the study by Claude Elwood Shannon (1948), communication theory has demarcated sender effects, medium effects, and receiver effects (see Katz 2001 for a review). The sender is the person trying to communicate, the medium is how they are communicating, and the receiver is the person to whom the communication is directed (Shannon and Weaver 1963). Each part of this three-step process has properties that make it more or less likely that the communication will affect the receiver (see Fiske 1982 for more on this point). Berlo (1960) finessed this model by separating the message from the sender. He noted that the receiver might have opinions about the sender separate from the actual message, which may moderate the influence. Berlo's contribution is often described as a Sender-Message-Channel-Receiver model, with each component having dozens of subcategories that have been subsequently studied. This theoretical literature underlies almost all communication effects research. Not only does it provide the basic building blocks for understanding how communication is influential, but it also provides excellent insight into understanding media effects.

However, it is essential to note that although the eventual impact of communication is typically assumed to be what the sender intended to convey, it is not necessarily so. Each step in the process has a range of possible mediating and moderating factors, and the impact may, in fact, not be what the sender intended. This point is crucial for my theory because the foundational research does not specify that the audience affected needs to be the speaker's intended audience.

Notice, also, that the level of impact of the message is not measured in this model. The Shannon and Weaver model only mechanically describes how communication happens. It does not specify the size or strength of the effects. The next step in communication science was to establish the degree to which communication is impactful, which leads to similar models of influence from the conditioning literature in psychology.

The Stimulus-Organism-Response Model

The causal model of communication effects I use in developing my theory derives from the Stimulus-Organism-Response (S-O-R) paradigm within psychology (see Bettman 1979 for a summary). This psychology research states that *stimulus*, *organism*, and *response* are the three elements in a reaction that may change beliefs or behaviors (Mehrabian and Russell 1974). The model is not substantially different from the Shannon and Weaver (1963) model, but here the sender effects are typically outweighed by the medium and receiver effects unless certain conditions are met.

The primary element is the organism, which encompasses the individual and all previous inputs underlying that person's current opinions about the issue at hand. In econometrics, one might think of this as the lag of the dependent variable. The stimulus would be the key independent variable in a standard regression model, to continue this econometrics metaphor. The final component is the response, which would be the dependent variable, to continue the econometrics metaphor. The S-O-R model has become the dominant paradigm that psychologists use to formulate whether an event impacts a person's beliefs or behavior. Communication science has adopted this model and has used it extensively to explain how communication may or may not impact behavior.

This model provides a psychological underpinning for the minimal effects paradigm, but it also shows the potential parameters by which communication could be influential. The critical issue is that the (O)rganism almost always outweighs any (S)timulus, so the expected effect from any new stimulus is minimal. Consequently, the response is also small, and the abbreviation s-O-r might reflect the relationship between these factors more accurately. Importantly for my theory, however, if an effect is expected, the stimulus would need to overwhelm the organism; that is, we would use the abbreviation S-o-R.

Thus, the most critical factor concerning communication is what the receiver believes about the topic before the communication. Of course, the more vivid, intense, and lengthy the sender's communication is, the more likely it will impact the receiver (Sherer and Rogers 1984). However, the stimulus will be filtered according to the prior beliefs of the organism. Even if the sender provides dramatic new information in a lengthy communication, influencing the receiver will be difficult if they have deeply held beliefs on the topic, do not believe the information, or are uninterested in the topic.

The S-O-R model is persuasive primarily due to its parsimony. It explains almost the entirety of communicative processes with only three variables. Nevertheless, each one of these variables has contingent sub-influences, which can number in the hundreds. The literature has found dozens of influences, for example, based on psychological predispositions to accept the messages within communication (Daly 1987). But the parsimony of the basic model allows clarity and understanding of what is influencing communication. This model serves as the basis for my primary theoretical model extrapolated below based on the Rescorla–Wagner model.

The Rescorla–Wagner Model

The research on conditioning in psychology collectively led to a major theoretical breakthrough, represented in the Rescorla–Wagner model (Rescorla and Wagner 1972):

$$\Delta V = \alpha \beta (\lambda - \Sigma V) \tag{1}$$

Here, V represents the stimulus, and ΔV is the change in the stimulus's level.[2] ΣV is the sum of the strengths of all stimuli present in the situation. λ is the maximum prior strength of the unconditioned stimuli. The model includes constants α and β for the reach and salience of the stimuli, respectively.

To expound on this model, I use the example of American identity and Trump's anti-immigration rhetoric. Most Americans citizens have some attachment to American identity, with only a small number having none. This attachment is the unconditioned stimuli set at their maximum level in λ. Attachment to American identity is affected by a combination of Trump's rhetoric and all other prior stimuli, which is summed in ΣV. The Trump rhetoric is the conditioned stimuli, and all other prior experiences and the discourse that altered the person's attachment to American identity are included in ΣV. The constants α and β represent whether the individual can be affected by the rhetoric and how much attention the person pays to the rhetoric. Using this model as a theoretical basis, I now formally state a theory of collateral damage in political communication.

A Theory of Collateral Damage in Political Communication

My theory is that political socialization is so profound for most Americans that presidential rhetoric will rarely be powerful enough to overcome decades of prior socialization processes. Because their parents were born in the United States, most Americans have had lifelong input through vast

---

2. See Rescorla and Wagner (1972) for a full explication of the formal model, including proofs.

socialization processes at home to the extent that their opinions about politics are near unmovable by subsequent political communication. However, second-generation Americans have had less political socialization from parental influences as their parents are empirically much less likely to be partisan or have as firmly held beliefs about America. Second-generation Americans' lower level of political socialization allows for potential effects that would not be present in Americans with more robust political socialization. In sum, the combination of the intensity of Trump's rhetoric with the lack of socialization of second-generation Americans into American political institutions creates an environment conducive for media effects to be larger than usual in American politics.

In creating my theory, I take the formal model from Equation 1 and extend it by adding elements from four lemmas serving as guidelines. I offer Equation 2 as a formal model of my theory. Note that it separates the key independent variable—here denoted by the variable R for Trump's rhetoric—from the summation of all other independent variables denoted by ΣV.

$$\Delta V = \alpha\beta(\lambda - R + \Sigma V) \tag{2}$$

This formal model of collateral damage in political rhetoric now gives a clear theoretical picture for when Trump's rhetoric could matter. We can expect rhetoric to be influential when it is distributed widely enough to reach a listener (α), who is paying attention (β), and the impact of prior independent variables is low in proportion to the maximum possible value of the dependent variable ($\lambda - \Sigma V \gg 0$). Finally, the direction and strength of the rhetoric (R) must be sufficiently larger than ΣV to have an impact. If α and β are approximately one, then the speaker's intention is irrelevant because the messaging has reached the potentially affected audience. If all these conditions are met, then the key independent variable will likely have an effect. Put in the academic language of communication science, the rhetoric will have a nonminimal effect.

Note that the message does not have to be intended to impact the receiver for it to do so in this theoretical model. The mere connection of the communication to the receiver—be it intended or not—is enough to have an effect as long as the other lemmas of the model hold; that is, α and $\beta \approx 1$ and $\lambda + R - \Sigma V < 0$. So, in this case, whether Trump was trying to denigrate second-generation Americans' commitment to the United States broadly or to the Republican Party is irrelevant. What matters is that they hear the message, pay attention to it, and the prior attitudes toward that message were not total in their effect. If change can occur, then intention plays no part in this theoretical model.

Of course, someone's true intention can never be determined because unspoken desires cannot be analyzed. Nevertheless, one could plausibly make assumptions about a candidate's desires to be elected (see Mayhew 1974). This assumption does not suggest that every action that Trump engages in is rational; it merely highlights that Trump has no specific reason to alienate this group. Also, note that if Trump has a base mobilization strategy designed to inflame conflict about immigration, that also does not assume or require that Trump simultaneously alienates second-generation Americans. It merely requires that it would be advantageous for him to rile up his base with anti-immigration rhetoric; it does not have any bearing on whether Trump *intended* to alienate second-generation Americans with his anti-immigration rhetoric.

Next, I discuss how this theory interacts with the anti-immigration rhetoric on ethnic subgroups.

Theoretical Expectations the Effect of Anti-Immigration Rhetoric on Subgroups

The theory of collateral damage also helps demonstrate why anti-immigration rhetoric may differentially impact specific subgroups, and it provides a clear picture of when this rhetoric could matter more for specific subpopulations. Equation 3 once more shows the theory:

$$\Delta V = \alpha\beta(\lambda - R + \Sigma V) \tag{3}$$

In examining the theory, we can see that for rhetoric to be influential, it requires that someone is paying attention (β) to what is being said and that the direction and strength of the rhetoric must be relatively large compared with the prior beliefs to have a sufficiently significant impact ($R + \Sigma V$).

Since Trump's rhetoric was focused on problems he claimed were created by undocumented immigration from Mexico, I expect this subpopulation to be disproportionately affected by his rhetoric through the following two processes. One of the critical lemmas regarding experiencing an impact from rhetoric is an interest in the topic of the rhetoric. I expect second-generation Mexican Americans to be more likely to be paying attention (β) to Trump's rhetoric because it is specifically about people like their families. In addition, because the rhetoric is so intense—including accusations that Mexican immigrants are rapists and killers, for example—I would expect that its direction and strength (R) are more potent for this subgroup so that it has a more significant impact on them.

The impact of Trump's rhetoric is potentially attenuated for Vietnamese Americans and Cuban Americans because their prior belief system, developed through political socialization, translates to greater support for the Republican Party. In effect, their prior beliefs about American politics are more crystallized than other immigrant subgroups, and thus loom larger in the model relative to Trump's rhetoric. Because the theory requires that the rhetoric be large in proportion to the prior beliefs about a topic, it subsequently predicts that people who have strong prior beliefs through political socialization processes will be less likely to be influenced by rhetoric (i.e., that R is not necessarily larger than ΣV). Because Cuban Americans rallied around the Republican Party due to its fierce stance against the Castro regime, Cuban Americans may have a deeper level of socialization into the American party system than other second-generation Americans. Similarly, many Vietnamese Americans responded to Ronald Reagan's anti-communism and tough stances on the Communist Party of Vietnam by identifying more often with the Republican Party. Thus, the theory predicts that these two subpopulations will be less likely to be affected by rhetoric because they already hold deeply ingrained partisan identification with the Republican Party.

The assumption that second-generation Americans do not have a thorough partisan identification is validated in chapter 6, with survey research showing that these Americans are not deeply tied to a particular political party. However, political socialization may be more common for specific subgroups within larger groupings of second-generation Americans. Decades of research on Cuban Americans and Vietnamese Americans have shown that a majority identified with the Republican Party and voted for the Republican Party's presidential nominee. Because of this attachment to the Republican Party, we can expect partisan motivated reasoning to influence their opinions about rhetoric similar to non-second-generation Americans who have had more extensive exposure and socialization within the American two-party system (see Hajnal and Lee 2011). Chapters 5 and 6 examine the general theory on second-generation Americans, while chapter 7 examines ethnic subgroups within the second generation.

In the next section, we examine the communication literature specifically about immigration.

Communication and Second-Generation Americans

The causal mechanisms that make political rhetoric influential on incorporation processes have only been discussed in a few articles in the United States and Europe. Primarily in the context of Latinos in the United States, the primary studies of the impact of anti-immigration political rhetoric were conducted by Efrén O. Pérez (2015a and 2015b). Pérez (2015a, 2015b) shows that anti-immigrant rhetoric can intensify in-group feelings and lower political trust. Both outcomes suggest that incorporation would be less likely. In Europe, anti-immigration rhetoric has sometimes not been influential in political incorporation (e.g., Wright and Bloemraad 2012). Nevertheless, Simonsen (2021) finds that second-generation immigrants living in countries with higher anti-immigrant elite rhetoric have less political trust and satisfaction with democracy. Stuckey (2004) shows that throughout American history, American presidents have defined "we the people" in terms of that would be politically beneficial to them, and often define who Americans are in exclusionary terms that would impact those trying to incorporate into America.

Determining the level of integration of second-generation Americans is essential for this research and theoretical model, so understanding these Americans' current state of integration is necessary. The current wave of immigration—perhaps the largest in US history—has been commonly found to integrate at least as fast as prior generations. Many native-born Americans, however, worry about the integration of immigrants (Schildkraut 2005). However, a large body of literature has established that despite deep concern about the integration of these Americans, their children integrate rapidly (see Branton 2007; Frank, Akresh, and Lu 2010). For example, Citrin et al. (2007) show across many measures that the high level of immigration is not leading to a situation whereby immigrants are not incorporating. Also, survey data clearly show that immigrants to the United States feel a deep attachment to this country and feel that they are a part of its political system (Pew Research Center 2013, 10).

Integration involves both the willingness of the immigrants to incorporate and the openness of the host society to accept them into the political realm. More importantly, this research must study whether the often hostile reaction to the recent large wave of immigrants creates a potential backlash against integration from this group. Intense anti-immigration rhetoric could plausibly make immigrants and their children less willing to integrate into the host society. Often the most vexing issue for those who oppose immigration is the supposed lack of integration of immigrants.

However, their rhetoric may itself be one of the factors that discourage immigrants from integrating. In this case, the opposition to immigration would lead to a self-fulfilling prophecy that immigrants do not wish to integrate into the broader society.

Still, significant evidence exists for discrimination against the immigrants and their children, which may lead them not to seek out full incorporation. For example, Frank, Redstone Akresh, and Lu (2010) find a significant difference in income for Hispanic immigrant workers versus native workers, even after controlling for differences in education and skills. Additionally, we know there has been a significant uptick in anti-immigration sentiment. Even though it may or may not be the result of the political rhetoric that I study in this book, it still could inhibit full integration (see Hainmueller and Hopkins 2014 for a recent review of literature on attitudes toward immigration). An extensive literature documents anti-immigrant sentiment in American politics (Brader, Valentino, and Suhay 2008; Citrin, Reingold, and Green 1990; Citrin et al. 1997; Fetzer 2000). This is particularly true if there is a large influx of immigrants and elite rhetoric is anti-immigrant (see also Hainmueller and Hiscox 2007).

In addition to elites' political rhetoric, day-to-day social networking may influence attitudes toward the United States and the Republican Party. Specifically, extensive literature exists on the impact of political discussion, which is profoundly influential across many methodologies. A related area of possible nonelite influence is churches, as many immigrants are involved in interethnic religious institutions, such as Protestant evangelical churches. Despite assumptions across academia about immigrants' desires, immigrants, in fact, commonly want to integrate into the dominant society.

In sum, there is much evidence to suggest that integration is proceeding as it has in prior eras. However, there is also evidence to suggest that the current political climate is inhospitable to the full incorporation of second-generation Americans. Because the level of integration is still in flux, it is crucial to have empirical analyses over what influences these processes.

Conclusion

Throughout its long history, communication science research has never suggested significant direct effects from political rhetoric. However, factors specific to second-generation Americans and the environment in which they live have created the potential for the effects of Trump's rhetoric to be nonminimal, as outlined in my theory explicated in Equation 2. The specific focus and intensity of Trump's rhetoric combined with the second-generation Americans' lack of long-term predetermined dispositions about American politics allow for the possibility of a significant effect. My theory suggests that a confluence of circumstances has produced an environment in which the impact of communication is plausibly more pronounced than typically exists in a fully developed democracy such as the United States.

I also theorized that Cuban, Vietnamese, and Mexican Americans would have unique factors that differentially influence these groups. In combination, this suggests a conditional impact from presidential rhetoric. Anti-immigration rhetoric will be more likely to influence those with less parental political socialization and differentiated by how members of these ethnicities have preconceived beliefs about America and these political parties. That is the conditional effects component of my theory.

I also more broadly theorize that there are profound influences on second-generation Americans who are US citizens. While they have had less political socialization than those who had parents born in America, they still have had some political socialization from education, the mass media, and other sources. This means that my theory would be that influence from presidential rhetoric is conditional on parental influence and ethnicity and limited by prior political socialization levels, which will not be absent completely for these US citizens.

In the next chapter I will examine the four previously stated lemmas necessary for my theory. I show in the subsequent chapter that the empirical evidence suggests that all four of the lemmas are valid.

References

Bennett, W. Lance, and Shanto Iyengar. 2008. "A New Era of Minimal Effects? The Changing Foundations of Political Communication." *Journal of Communication* 58 (4): 707–31.

Ben-Porath, Sigal. 2006. *Citizenship under Fire: Democratic Education in Times of Conflict*. Princeton: Princeton University Press.

Berelson, Bernard, Paul F. Lazarsfeld, and William N. McPhee. 1954. *Voting*. Chicago: University of Chicago Press.

Berlo, David. 1960. *The Process of Communication*. New York: Holt, Rinehart & Winston.

Bettman, James R. 1979. *An Information Processing Theory of Consumer Choice*. Reading, MA: Addison-Wesley.

Brader, Ted, Nicholas A. Valentino, and Elizabeth Suhay. 2008. "What Triggers Public Opposition to Immigration? Anxiety, Group Cues, and Immigration Threat." *American Journal of Political Science* 52 (4): 959–78.

Branton, Regina. 2007. "Latino Attitudes toward Various Areas of Public Policy: The Importance of Acculturation." *Political Research Quarterly* 60 (2): 293–303.
Brighouse, Harry. 2005. *On Education: Thinking in Action*. London: Routledge Press.
Campbell, Karlyn Kohrs, and Kathleen Hall Jamieson. 1990. *Deeds Done in Words: Presidential Rhetoric and the Genres of Governance*. Chicago: University of Chicago Press.
Canes-Wrone, Brandice. 2005. *Who Leads Whom? Presidents, Policy Making, and the Mass Public*. Chicago: University of Chicago Press.
Citrin, Jack, Donald P. Green, Christopher Muste, and Cara Wong. 1997. "Public Opinion toward Immigration Reform: The Role of Economic Motivations." *Journal of Politics* 59 (3): 858–81.
Citrin, Jack, Amy Lerman, Michael Murakami, and Kathryn Pearson. 2007. "Testing Huntington: Is Hispanic Immigration a Threat to American Identity?" *Perspectives on Politics* 5 (1): 31–48.
Citrin, Jack, Beth Reingold, and Donald P. Green. 1990. "American Identity and the Politics of Ethnic Change." *Journal of Politics* 52 (4): 1124–54.
Cohen, Jeff E. 2008. *The Presidency in the Era of 24-Hour News*. Princeton: Princeton University Press.
Cohen, Jeff E. 2010. *Going Local: Presidential Leadership in the Post-Broadcast Age*. Cambridge: Cambridge University Press.
Daly, John. 1987. "Personality and Interpersonal Communication." In *Personality and Interpersonal Communication*, edited by John A. Daly and James C. McCroskey. Beverly Hills, CA: Sage Press.
Druckman, James N., and Justin W. Holmes. 2004. "Does Presidential Rhetoric Matter? Priming and Presidential Approval." *Presidential Studies Quarterly* 34 (4): 755–78.
Easton, David. 1975. "A Re-Assessment of the Concept of Political Support." *British Journal of Political Science* 5 (4): 435–57.
Edwards, George. 2003. *On Deaf Ears: The Limits of the Bully Pulpit*. New Haven: Yale University Press.
Eshbaugh-Soha, Matthew. 2008. "Local Newspaper Coverage of the Presidency." *International Journal of Press/Politics* 13 (2): 103–19.
Eshbaugh-Soha, Matthew, and Jeffrey S. Peake. 2011. *Breaking Through the Noise: Presidential Leadership, Public Opinion, and the News Media*. Stanford: Stanford University Press.
Eshbaugh-Soha, Matthew, and Brandon Rottinghaus. 2013. "Presidential Position Taking and the Puzzle of Representation." *Presidential Studies Quarterly* 43 (1): 1–15.
Fetzer, Joel S. 2000. *Public Attitudes toward Immigration in the United States, France, and Germany*. New York: Cambridge University Press.
Fiske, John. 1982. *Introduction to Communication Studies*. London: Routledge Press.
Frank, Reanne, Ilana Redstone Akresh, and Bo Lu. 2010. "Latino Immigrants and the US Racial Order: How and Where Do They Fit In?" *American Sociological Review* 75 (3): 370–401.
Hainmueller, Jens, and Michael J. Hiscox. 2007. "Educated Preferences: Explain-

ing Attitudes toward Immigration in Europe." *International Organization* 61 (2): 399–442.
Hainmueller, Jens, and Daniel J. Hopkins. 2014. "Public Attitudes toward Immigration." *Annual Review of Political Science* 17 (1): 225–49.
Hajnal, Zoltan, and Taeku Lee. 2011. *Why Americans Don't Join the Party: Race, Immigration, and the Failure (of Political Parties) to Engage the Electorate*. Princeton: Princeton University Press.
Huntington, Samuel. 2004. *Who Are We? The Challenges to America's National Identity*. New York: Simon & Shuster.
Iyengar, Shanto, and Donald R. Kinder. 1987. *News That Matters: Television and American Opinion*. Chicago: University of Chicago Press.
Iyengar, Shanto, Mark D. Peters, and Donald R. Kinder. 1982. "Experimental Demonstrations of the 'Not-So-Minimal' Consequences of Television News Programs." *American Political Science Review* 76 (4): 848–58.
Jacobs, Lawrence R., and Robert Y. Shapiro. 2000. *Politicians Don't Pander: Political Manipulation and the Loss of Democratic Responsiveness*. Chicago: University of Chicago Press.
Karp, Jeffrey A., and Susan A Banducci. 2008. "Political Efficacy and Participation in Twenty-Seven Democracies: How Electoral Systems Shape Political Behaviour." *British Journal of Political Science* 38 (2): 311–34.
Katz, Elihu. 1957. "The Two-Step Flow of Communication: An Up-to-Date Report on a Hypothesis." *Public Opinion Quarterly* 21 (1): 61–78.
Katz, Elihu. 2001. "Media Effects." In *International Encyclopedia of the Social & Behavioral Sciences*, edited by Neil J. Smelser and Paul B. Baltes, 9472–79. Oxford: Elsevier.
Kernell, Samuel. 1986. *Going Public: New Strategies of Presidential Leadership*. Washington, DC: CQ Press.
Klapper, Joseph T. 1960. *The Effects of Mass Communication*. New York: Free Press.
Lazarsfeld, Paul F., Bernard Berelson, and Hazel Gaudet. 1944. *The People's Choice: How the Voter Makes Up His Mind in a Presidential Campaign*. New York: Columbia University Press.
Logan, Jessica, L. Justice, M. Yumuş, and L. J. Chaparro-Moreno. 2019. "When Children Are Not Read to at Home: The Million Word Gap." *Journal of Developmental and Behavioral Pediatrics* 40 (5): 383–86.
Mayhew, David. 1974. *Congress: The Electoral Connection*. Clinton, MA: Colonial Press.
Mehrabian, Albert, and James A. Russell. 1974. *An Approach to Environmental Psychology*. Cambridge, MA: MIT Press.
Ostrom, Elinor. 1998. "A Behavioral Approach to the Rational Choice Theory of Collective Action." *American Political Science Review* 92 (1): 389–97.
Pérez, Efrén O. 2015a. "Xenophobic Rhetoric and Its Political Effects on Immigrants and Their Co-Ethnics." *American Journal of Political Science* 59 (3): 549–64.
Pérez, Efrén O. 2015b. "Ricochet: How Elite Discourse Politicizes Racial and Ethnic Identities." *Political Behavior* 37 (1): 155–80.

Pew Research Center. 2013. *Second-Generation Americans: A Portrait of the Adult Children of Immigrants.* https://www.pewsocialtrends.org/wp-content/uploads/sites/3/2013/02/FINAL_immigrant_generations_report_2-7-13.pdf

Rescorla, R. A., and Allan R. Wagner. 1972. "A Theory of Pavlovian Conditioning: Variations in the Effectiveness of Reinforcement and Nonreinforcement." In *Classical Conditioning II: Current Research and Theory,* edited by Abraham H. Black and William F. Prokasy, 64–99. New York: Appleton Century Crofts.

Scacco, Joshua, and Kevin Coe. 2016. "The Ubiquitous Presidency: Toward a New Paradigm for Studying Presidential Communication." *International Journal of Communication* 10: 2014–37.

Schildkraut, Deborah J. 2005. *Press One for English: Language Policy, Public Opinion, and American Identity.* Princeton: Princeton University Press.

Shannon, Claude Elwood. 1948. "A Mathematical Theory of Communication." *Bell System Technical Journal* 27 (3): 379–423.

Shannon, Claude E., and Warren Weaver. 1963. *The Mathematical Theory of Communication.* Urbana: University of Illinois Press.

Sherer, Mark, and Ronald W. Rogers. 1984. "The Role of Vivid Information in Fear Appeals and Attitude Change." *Journal of Research in Personality* 18 (3): 321–34.

Simonsen, Kristina Bakkær. 2021. "The Democratic Consequences of Anti-immigrant Political Rhetoric: A Mixed Methods Study of Immigrants' Political Belonging." *Political Behavior* 43 (1): 143–74.

Simonson, Peter. 2014. "The Rise and Fall of the Limited Effects Model." In *The International Encyclopedia of Media Studies,* edited by Angharad N. Valdivia. London: John Wiley & Sons.

Stuckey, Mary E. 2004. *Defining Americans: The Presidency and National Identity.* Lawrence: University Press of Kansas.

Tedin, Kent, Brandon Rottinghaus, and Harrell Rodgers. 2010. "When the President Goes Public: The Consequences of Communication Mode for Opinion Change across Issue Types and Groups." *Political Research Quarterly* 64 (3): 506–19.

Torcal, Mariano, and José Ramón Montero. 2006. *Political Disaffection in Contemporary Democracies: Social Capital, Institutions and Politics.* London: Routledge Press.

Tulis, Jeffrey K. 1987. *The Rhetorical Presidency.* Princeton: Princeton University Press.

Whipple, Mark. 2005. "The Dewey-Lippmann Debate Today: Communication Distortions, Reflective Agency, and Participatory Democracy." *Sociological Theory* 23 (2): 156–78.

Whorf, Benjamin Lee. 1940. "Science and Linguistics." *Technology Review* 42: 221–31, 247–48.

Wright, Matthew, and Irene Bloemraad. 2012. "Is There a Trade-Off between Multiculturalism and Socio-Political Integration? Policy Regimes and Immigrant Incorporation in Comparative Perspective." *Perspectives on Politics* 10 (1): 77–95.

CHAPTER 3

Conditions Necessary for Collateral Damage

I need to demonstrate that the four lemmas described in chapter 2 are empirically valid to test my theory. Specifically, I need to show that the media covered Donald Trump's anti-immigration rhetoric enough that most second-generation Americans were exposed to it (lemma 1). Also, I need to show that the children of immigrants are attuned to anti-immigration rhetoric because they care about immigrants (lemma 2). I also need to demonstrate that the children of immigrants can be influenced on the topics mentioned in the rhetoric because they are not highly socialized into beliefs about the United States or its party system (lemma 3). Finally, evidence is needed to show that the effect is not dependent on Trump's intention (lemma 4). In this chapter, I provide empirical support for each of these four lemmas.

Based on a content analysis of newspaper coverage, I find that the level of Donald Trump's anti-immigration rhetoric—as well as the level of media coverage of it—was unique compared with prior presidential elections and Republican nominees. I then show that second-generation Americans were interested in immigration during this election at a higher level than ever before and that they cared more about undocumented immigrants (the primary group that Trump disparages) than non-second-generation Americans. Third, I show that research on second-generation Americans' political socialization shows that they are not so firmly attached to either an American identity[1] or the Republican Party that they are not persuad-

---

1. Emerson (1960) provides a helpful definition of national identity as "a body of people who feel that they are a nation" (Emerson 1960, 3). In this research, I am testing how anti-immigrant rhetoric affects this feeling of shared togetherness in one nation.

able to change. Fourth, and most difficult, I provide evidence that Trump did not expressly desire or gain from preventing immigrant incorporation but instead was probably bashing immigrants for other purposes.

Overall, I show that Trump's anti-immigration rhetoric was more extensive than rhetoric on the same topic in the past, and media coverage was widespread. I also show that second-generation Americans care deeply about immigration as a topic and are not deeply intertwined with America or its political parties. Given these findings, Trump's rhetoric may have had an unintended disproportionate and profoundly negative impact on this subpopulation.

These results provide fundamental support for my theory of how unintended communication effects still have transformative impacts on interested subpopulations.

Lemma 1: Establishing That Coverage of Trump's Rhetoric Was Widespread

Since the country's founding, American politics has featured anti-immigration rhetoric, but such rhetoric was a central issue in 2016 as it had never been before. The United States has never had a presidential candidate like Trump in terms of rhetoric on immigration, and the negative opinions of second-generation Americans toward Republican presidents or presidential nominees are also unprecedented. Furthermore, while many citizens may believe that Trump's rhetoric is anti-immigrant, it is necessary to establish that empirically. Harsh campaign rhetoric is the impetus for this book's research because of its intense focus on immigration's negative aspects. This focus is shown both through media coverage of Trump's rhetoric and the attitudes of second-generation Americans. The evidence that I present in chapters 3 and 4 clearly and unequivocally shows that Trump is distinct from prior presidents in using his platform to disparage immigrants, which leads to the need for empirical research that demonstrates how the rhetoric he uses affects the people who care about the issue of immigration, such as the children of immigrants.

Since immigrant-bashing has a long history in American politics, it may be tempting to think that saying this many negative things against immigrants has been commonplace throughout history. The first step toward showing that Trump's presidency has the hypothesized impact is demonstrating that coverage of his rhetoric is profoundly different from prior Republican presidential candidates and presidents. My approach involves conducting a content analysis of US newspapers that centers on anti-immigration phrases and Republican candidates (Macnamara 2005). The newspapers that I sample from are every American newspaper that is contained in the internet database LexisNexis. Content analysis based on newspapers is a commonly used and well-validated methodology in political communication research (Neuendorf 2002).

The advantage of this approach is that the historical record on newspapers is a long one (Weber 1990). Additionally, we can expect that newspaper coverage of presidential candidates has historically been robust. As such, the anti-immigration rhetoric that a presidential candidate has publicly delivered will be well documented. Stryker et al. (2006) examine the validity of newspaper coverage compared to other forms of media and show that it resembles other forms of communication as well. Based on the long literature showing the validity of using newspaper coverage to measure general media content, I examine newspaper coverage of Trump, Republicans, and immigration.

My content analysis was based on LexisNexis, a database containing a digitized copy of almost every newspaper article from most American newspapers going back decades. Figure 1 shows the results of my search in LexisNexis for all mentions of *immigration* going back to 1984.[2] The use of the word from 2000 onward, particularly in the last decade, shows the increasing salience of immigration as a topic in the media and suggests its primary importance in current American politics. The latter point is intuitive to anyone who follows American politics, but it is necessary to prove for my argument to empirically demonstrate that the American public has been broadly exposed to articles on immigration. Since other empirical research has demonstrated that newspaper topics also receive television and radio news coverage (e.g., Weber 1990), we can assume that newspaper articles are representative of the larger media landscape and immigration is a highly salient and well-covered topic throughout that landscape.

Notably, after Trump was nominated as the Republican presidential candidate, an explosion of usage of the word immigration occurred in American newspapers, strongly suggesting that his candidacy significantly increased focus on this topic.

The same methodological technique was used to produce figure 2, but the presidential candidate's name for the Republican Party was simultaneously added to the search with the word immigration for each presidential

---

2. The search criteria for this used the word "immigration," not case sensitive, from January 1, 1984, until December 31, 2018. All the subsequent content analysis in this chapter uses similar search criteria.

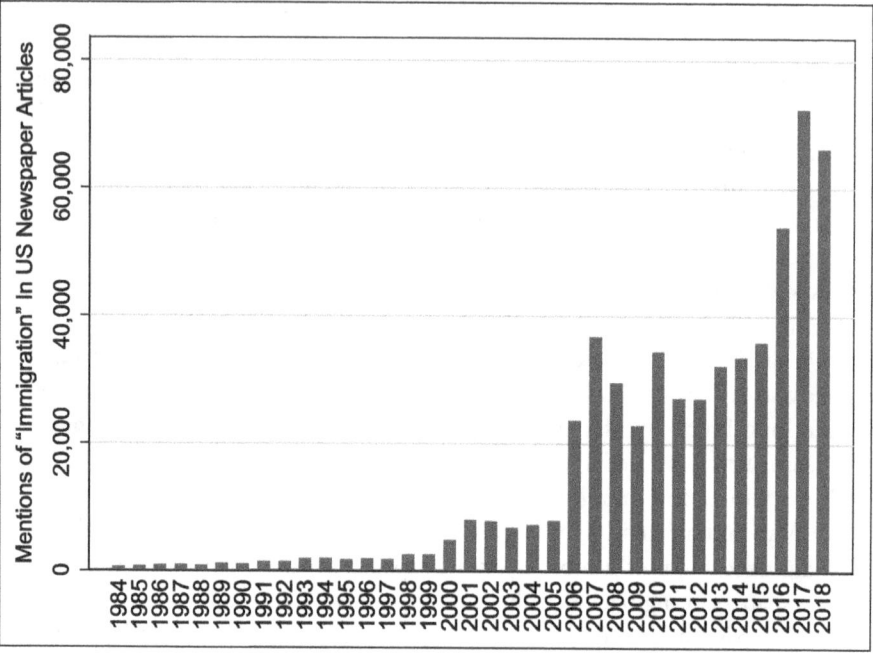

Fig. 1. Number of mentions of "immigration" in US newspaper articles from 1984 to 2018. The number of mentions of "immigration" in US newspaper articles from 1984 to 2018 has greatly increased, especially around 2016.

election year. For example, the search for articles from 1984 contained the words *Reagan* and *immigration*, whereas, for 1988, the search used *Bush* and *immigration*. The graph shows that the 2016 and 2020 elections stand out concerning how media coverage primed the presidential nominee of the Republican Party with immigration.

Although a slight increase occurred in 2000, mentions of the topic connected to the Republican candidate decreased slightly in 2008 and 2012. At first glance, this might be surprising because the base of the Republican Party was strongly anti-immigrant during the time, as shown by strict anti-immigration legislation being enacted at the state level in Arizona in 2010, opposition to policies such as comprehensive immigration reform, and hostile rhetoric from many politicians such as Steve King. Nevertheless, the Republican nominees in these years—John McCain and Mitt Romney—had relatively softer rhetoric on immigration and were generally considered more moderate on this topic than the more extreme parts

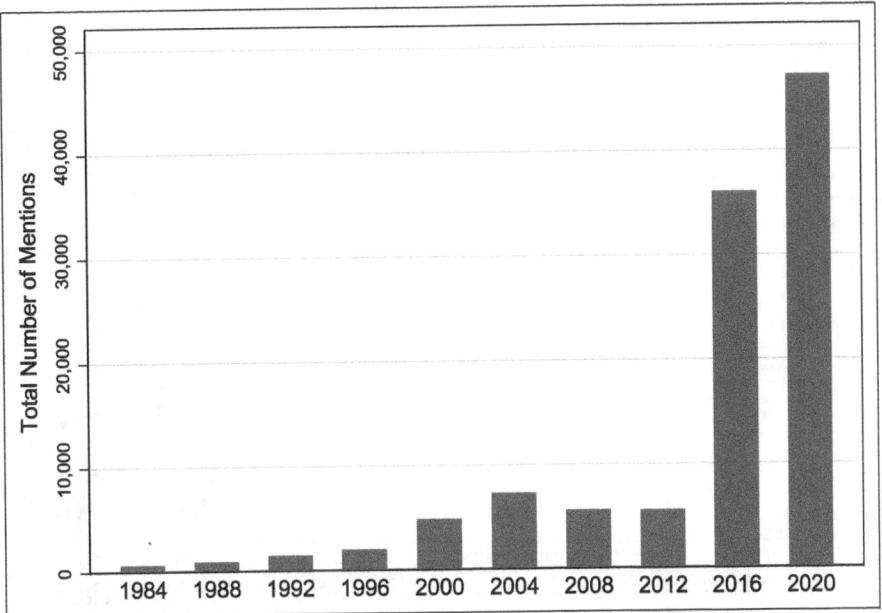

Fig. 2. Number of mentions of "immigration" and the last name of the Republican Party nominee for president in US newspaper articles in presidential election years, from 1984 to 2018.

of their party. Consequently, there was not as much newspaper coverage of candidates in connection with immigration. However, this situation changed dramatically with the nomination of Trump in 2016 and his reelection campaign in 2020. We see that unless the nominee used strong anti-immigration rhetoric, the priming of the two was not made in the mass media. The surge in coverage clearly shows the intensity with which Trump's rhetoric was covered in the media.

To get a more fine-grained analysis, I altered my search terms to specifically study whether the term *anti-immigration* appeared with the word *Republican* in newspaper articles. As shown in figure 3, articles in the 1980s had almost no pairing of the Republican Party and anti-immigration feelings, but such pairing quickly rose to a high level in the 2000s. After Trump initiated his bid for the presidency in 2015, it increased even more, peaking in 2016. One might imagine that the Republican Party has been associated with anti-immigration feelings since at least Pete Wilson's campaign for governor in California in the 1990s—which was based on an

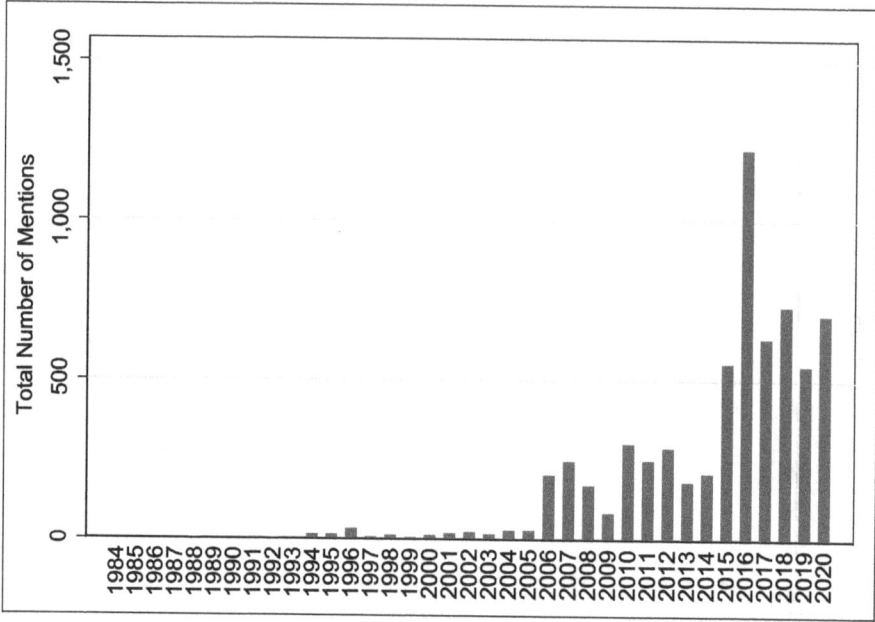

Fig. 3. Number of mentions of "anti-immigration" and "Republican" in the same US newspaper articles from 1984 to 2018.

anti-immigration platform—yet most newspaper coverage of this connection does not begin until the 2006 protests and movements for and against the comprehensive immigration bill of that year. After 2006, it is more common for a newspaper article to mention Republicans and the term anti-immigration.

Even more interesting is that figure 4 shows that Trump is not historically associated with anti-immigration rhetoric. This finding suggests that Trump's hardline rhetoric might have been an opportunistic campaign tactic rather than a deeply held long-term belief. A LexisNexis search uncovered no mention of Trump paired with the term anti-immigration from 1984 until 2012, despite his ongoing coverage on television and in newspapers throughout this entire period. He often spoke about politics, frequently railing against the United Nations and trade with Japan. He may have had anti-immigration beliefs during this period, but the media did not cover those beliefs at the same level as his other political views. Whether Trump was opportunistically taking advantage of the Republican

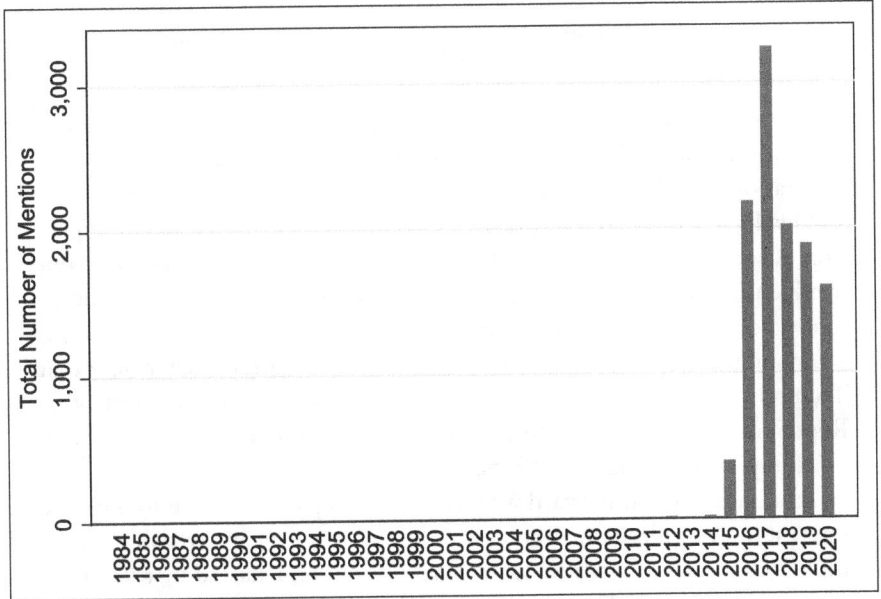

Fig. 4. Number of joint mentions of "anti-immigration" and "Trump" in US newspaper articles from 1984 to 2018.

Party base's anti-immigration feelings to win the nomination or whether he genuinely held these beliefs could not be determined with certainty. However, the evidence suggests at least some opportunism in his rhetoric.

Altogether, the evidence strongly indicates that the first lemma is correct: the media consistently and frequently covered Trump's anti-immigration rhetoric since 2015, and chapter 4 shows that this rhetoric was profoundly different from prior Republican rhetoric on immigration. The first part is necessary to conclude that Trump's rhetoric would negatively affect the incorporation of second-generation Americans. The second part shows that 2016 was different regarding Trump's rhetoric being unprecedented in US politics. The coverage of the rhetoric was widespread enough that any interested party would have delineated that the Republican nominee was using anti-immigration rhetoric in a way that had never happened before in American politics. Therefore, it potentially had an impact on those who care about the issue of immigration.

Lemma 2: Second-Generation Americans Were Attuned to Trump's Rhetoric in 2016

The second lemma necessary for the theory to be plausible is that second-generation Americans are interested in this topic. By showing that second-generation Americans care about immigrants, I can demonstrate that they will likely be attuned to rhetoric that pertains to immigrants and immigration. Also, examining the attitudes of second-generation Americans about presidential nominees over time can reveal whether the negative opinions voiced by nominees about immigrants influenced the way they view the nominees. If both facts can be established, I can then determine that Trump's candidacy and presidency are significantly different from prior Republican presidential rhetoric. This finding would justify a closer study of Trump's rhetoric and its effects.

The most straightforward way to test the impact would be to measure interest in Trump's rhetoric precisely, but no such data are available on the topic for second-generation Americans. Therefore, I started by examining the interest of second-generation Americans[3] in presidential elections by year and assessed whether they were more interested in the 2016 and 2020 presidential elections than in previous presidential elections. Based on data from the American National Election Study (ANES) time series, which measures interest in every presidential election from 1952 onward, figure 5 shows that second-generation Americans had more significant interest in the 2016 and 2020 presidential elections, more than any other prior election. I examined interest in the 2016 and 2020 elections for second-generation Americans compared with their interest level in prior presidential elections when Trump was not on the ballot. The pairwise correlation is 0.169, and the p-value is <.000, showing a significant correlation of more

---

3. Every two years since 1980, the ANES has asked where the respondents' parents were born. I coded respondents that had two foreign-born parents as second-generation Americans. This allowed comparing changes in the attitudes of second-generation Americans over time. The number of respondents from the second-generation population was based on their general population incidence rate because the samples were random. In no ANES survey does the number of second-generation American respondents ever exceed around 200. It is possible that since these samples were not directly designed to oversample second-generation Americans, some bias exists in the representativeness of these data.

Nevertheless, this data set is the best available information because the survey asked essential questions about politics from this often-ignored population over an extended time frame. The traditional phone surveys from which the data are derived have well-established validity. These samples were primarily face-to-face surveys with a high response rate, and they are considered the gold standard in political science. Indeed, prominent academic literature has been based on using these freely available data.

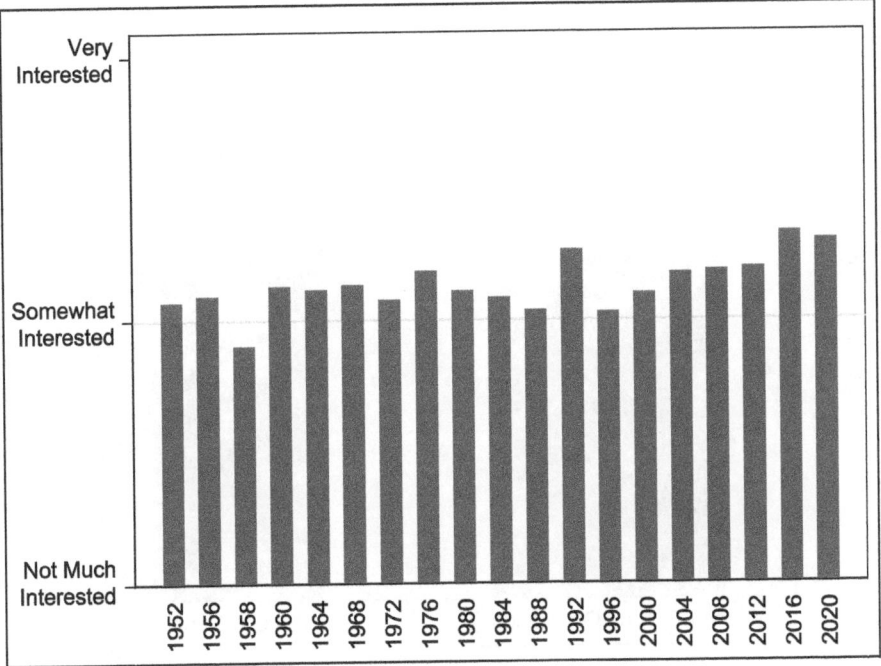

Fig. 5. Interest in presidential elections from second-generation Americans from the ANES survey (1952–2020).

interest when Trump was on the ballot in the 2016 and 2020 elections compared to 1952–2012. This equates to about 1/6th of a standard deviation increase in interest compared with the average interest for prior elections in this group. Of course, it is important not to overstate the results because there are still around half of second-generation Americans who do not care about the elections. Based on this result, we know that this group was paying more attention to elections when Trump was on the ballot.

The next step was to examine whether second-generation Americans care about undocumented immigrants, the topic of Trump's rhetoric. The ANES data from 2016 clearly show that second-generation Americans disproportionately care about undocumented immigrants. I started by measuring general feelings on a scale of 0 to 100, called feeling thermometers. The closer to 100, the more the respondent likes the person or group; the closer to 0, the more they dislike them. Figure 6 displays a thermometer measurement system based on a scale of 0 to 100, with higher numbers signaling warmer feelings toward them. Feelings toward

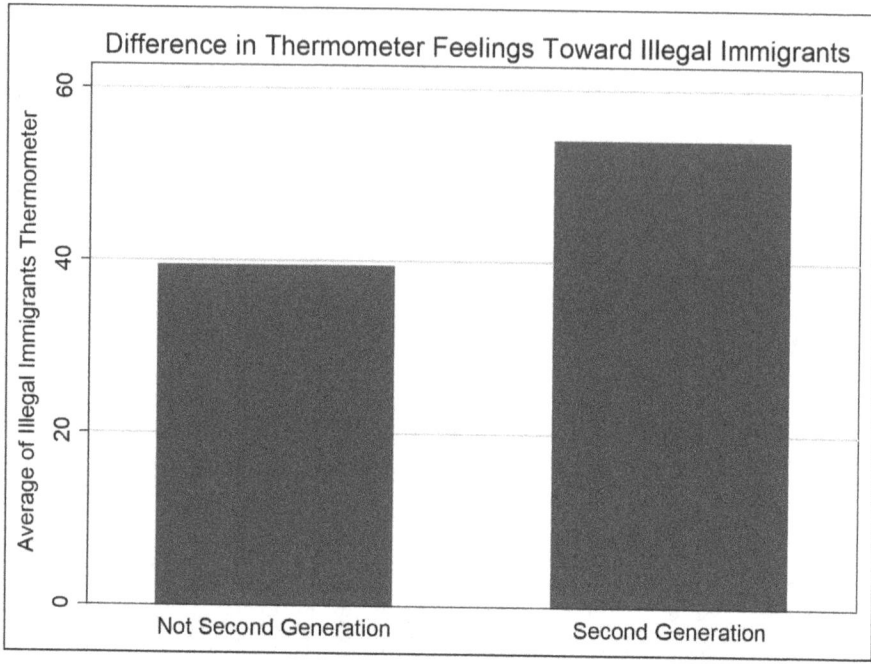

Fig. 6. Average feeling thermometer ratings for illegal immigrants for non-second-generation and second-generation Americans in the 2016 ANES survey.

groups are often measured this way in political science. Figure 6 shows that second-generation Americans' feelings toward undocumented immigrants (54.1%) were about 15 percentage points warmer than non-second-generation Americans (39.5%). The pairwise correlation is 0.178, and the *p*-value is <.000, showing a reasonably strong correlation between being a second-generation American and having warm feelings toward undocumented immigrants. This finding is crucial for showing why Trump's rhetoric would affect second-generation Americans, given that they disproportionately care about the group that he attacks.

Second-generation Americans' demographic background may differ from non-second-generation Americans, which may underlie variation in attitudes toward undocumented immigrants. Therefore, I used an ordinary least squares regression model for further analysis, controlling for demographic variables, and it produced similar results to the bivariate correlation. As shown in table 1, the correlation between second-generation Americans and the warmth of feelings for undocumented immigrants holds even after standard demographic variables are controlled.

TABLE 1. Feeling Thermometer Scores for Illegal Immigrants

Variable	Coef.	Std. Err
Second generation	8.077***	1.721
Education	3.695***	.462
Age	−0.119***	.027
Asian	−1.493	2.982
Hispanic	18.439***	1.882
Male	−1.907*	.944
Income	−0.225***	.065
Intercept	37.215***	2.035
N	3,140	
R^2	0.0833	

Source: Data from 2016 ANES survey.
$*p < .05, **p < .01, ***p < .001$

Another step toward building evidence for lemma 2 is examining whether second-generation Americans have more intense reactions to Trump than to prior Republican nominees. If so, the finding implies that they may be more affected by his rhetoric. The subject is difficult to test directly, but it is possible to draw inferences from the ANES data on second-generation American's opinions about various topics related to Trump. If survey data show that in 2016 their feelings of support for the Republican nominee were lower and their feelings of fear or being afraid of the Republican nominee were greater, it is possible that his anti-immigration rhetoric explains the difference, given that it is an area of substantial differences from previous Republican nominees.

One benefit of using nationally representative survey data over decades is that we can test data over time in a way that one-time experiments cannot. Additionally, although we try to get samples as nationally representative as possible in the experiments presented below, internet samples are new and potentially biased in some unknown way. Using nationally representative survey data shows more generalizability in the results.

Figure 7 shows changes in second-generation Americans' feelings toward the Republican presidential nominees over time. Figure 7 shows a distinct drop in thermometer feelings for when Trump was the nominee. These data alone do not prove that negative feelings toward him were due to his anti-immigration rhetoric, but they establish a need to explore why they were so low.

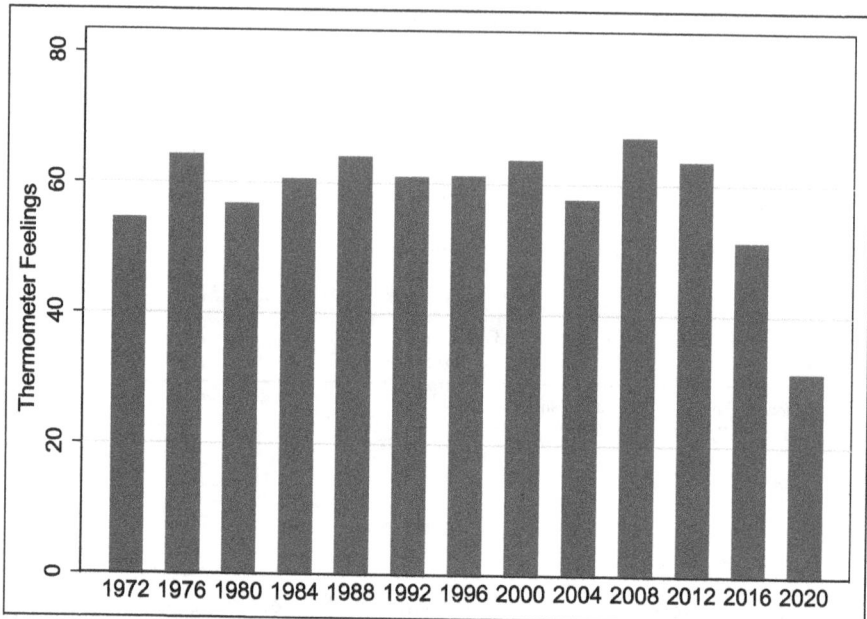

Fig. 7. Thermometer feelings of second-generation Americans toward republican presidential nominees, 1968 to 2016. ANES data.

Thermometer Feelings toward Republican Presidential Nominees

Relatedly, an extensive literature in political psychology shows that emotions such as fear or anger can generate attitudes and behavioral outcomes directly related to how a person feels toward politicians. Using ANES data from 1980 to 2016,[4] I measured the percentage of second-generation Americans who felt angry about or afraid of Republican presidential nominees. These emotions may have been due to simple partisan animus whereby Democrats and independents express negative feelings toward any Republican president because they are not identified with that party. To measure Trump's specific unique influence, separate from Republicanism in general, we can look at attitudes toward Republican presidential nominees over time. If Trump provoked greater anger and fear levels, my central hypothesis gains support; that is, second-generation Americans will be less likely to want to incorporate into the country and the Republican Party because it elected Trump.

---

4. Unfortunately, the ANES survey in 2020 did not include these questions.

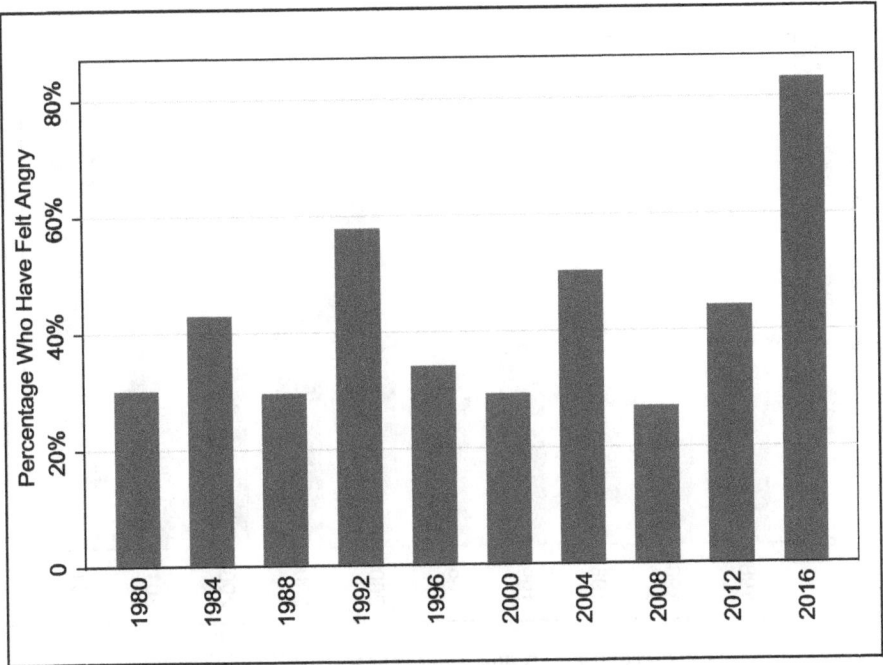

Fig. 8. Angry feelings of second-generation Americans toward Republican presidential nominees, 1980 to 2016. ANES data.

Figure 6 indicates that since 1980 no presidential candidate from the Republican Party has ever provoked as much anger from second-generation Americans as Trump. Eighty-three percent of second-generation Americans reported that they felt anger toward Trump during the 2016 election. The only other president about whom a majority of second-generation Americans said they felt anger was George H. W. Bush in 1992. With around 80% of second-generation Americans feeling angry about Trump at least once during the election, he clearly elicited disproportionately negative feelings about his nomination. As previously noted, this finding does not indicate that anger was explicitly about his anti-immigration rhetoric. For testing more nuanced causal mechanisms, I turn to experiments in subsequent chapters whereby I have more control over what is being tested. Nevertheless, the evidence presented here clearly demonstrates that Trump is different from prior candidates, supporting lemma 2.

Figure 9 shows that since 1980 the Republican presidential nominee that instilled the most fear by far in second-generation Americans was Trump. In 2004, around 40% of second-generation Americans feared

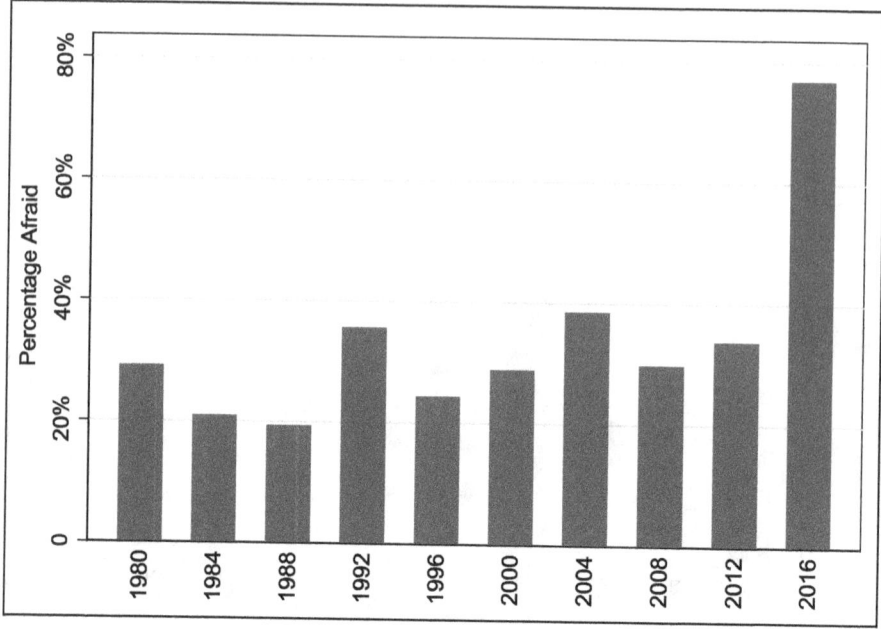

Fig. 9. Fear among second-generation Americans toward Republican presidential nominees, 1980 to 2016. ANES data.

George W. Bush, but no other Republican has even come close to eliciting as large an amount of fear as Trump did in 2016.

These results show that the data support lemma 2. Second-generation Americans were more interested in the presidential election of 2016 than any prior one in the period that was measured. They also had much warmer feelings than non-second-generation Americans toward undocumented immigrants. They were less warm toward Trump and angrier and more afraid of him than any prior Republican nominee. In sum, these results show that Trump's 2016 campaign made second-generation Americans disproportionately interested, afraid, and angry about his candidacy, which shows strong support for lemma 2.

Lemma 3: Attitudes Are Changeable

Research in political socialization underscores the family's primacy in establishing long-term party identification and general views about America. The research on this topic, which dates to the 1940s, has consistently shown that parents are the key drivers of political beliefs for most people (e.g., Lazarsfeld, Berelson, and Gaudet 1944). Although a stochastic probabilistic distribution exists whereby some people disagree with their parents, and some parents disagree with each other, the correlation with family is higher than any other variable in predicting a long-term association with a political party or beliefs about America (Jennings and Niemi 1968).

Notably, socialization can also mean not having a long-term relationship with a political party or establishing an American identity. If parents do not have a party identification, never speak about politics, and do not vote in elections, their children may infer that these topics are not worthy of their time or are not for people like them. As such, political socialization includes not having a party identification or a deeply ingrained sense of American identity as possible outcomes. Therefore, parents who do not have a party identification themselves or are not attached to an American identity are likely to pass on a similar belief system and general lack of incorporation into American political identities to their children.

Also, parents implicitly convey a general set of beliefs and values to their children. While these fundamental values derive from religion and other tenets of morality, their communication chiefly comes from the parents. From these core principles, children later develop positions on policies that will travel through the funnel of causality and eventually lead to party identification. For example, the authoritarian personality trait has a long, rich history in social science (Altemeyer 1981). Research shows that parental style—which includes factors such as whether parents use physical punishment—has a massive influence on how children later view society as adults (Stenner 2005). Authoritarians, who typically have strict parents who used physical punishment, are more supportive of the death penalty and harsher punishment for crime and generally more opposed to redistributive programs and help for minorities (Altemeyer 1981). These traits lead individuals with an authoritarian personality to be much more likely to support the Republican Party (Altemeyer 1981). Note that parenting style is not necessarily intended to influence ideology and partisan support, but it still ends up doing so.

Second-generation Americans likely experience implicit influence from their parents on fundamental values but little explicit influence concerning party politics. Consequently, the children of immigrants are less likely to perceive explicit parental support for any party. As such, second-generation Americans can be expected to have core beliefs shaped by their parents that will influence their ideology but not directly attach them to a specific political party. First-generation immigrants tend to have fragile partisan attachments, if any at all (Ramakrishnan 2005). Wong (2000) found that immigrants acquire partisan attachment after being in the United States for more extended periods, speaking English better, and having more exposure to political media.

Additionally, decades of research demonstrate that tying ideological beliefs and policy support to a party is not as simple as it may seem at first (e.g., Converse 1964). We have known since the 1940s that even most native-born Americans are disinterested in politics and have trouble expressing coherent ideological beliefs that coalesce around analytical support for the party that most closely matches those beliefs (Lazarsfeld, Berelson, and Gaudet 1944). This circumstance raises the question of how second-generation Americans develop partisan attachment.

Hajnal and Lee (2011) conducted an in-depth study of the relationship between immigrant identity and party identification. They argued that identity, ideology, and information influence party identification. The Republican Party's turn toward harsh anti-immigration rhetoric attacks a primary group identity of second-generation Americans. Due to the perception of linked fate (see chapter 6), second-generation Americans care deeply about immigrants. Also, because second-generation immigrants have less firmly attached partisan identification, they may be more receptive to rejecting a political party than other Americans. We know that "politics matter" in the sense that events and rhetoric experienced in youth have a profound lifelong impact on attitudes (see Sears and Valentino 1997; and also Sears and Funk 1999). Due to a lack of political socialization, there exists the possibility of an adverse reaction of second-generation Americans in the form of a rejection of the Republican Party due to Trump's rhetoric.

Some literature already supports parts of this proposition. For example, Ramakrishnan and Espenshade (2001) found that living in an area with anti-immigrant legislation leads to greater political participation by second-generation Americans. Also, Pantoja, Ramírez, and Segura (2001) showed that living during a period of anti-immigration rhetoric fosters immigrants' political action. Alvarez and García Bedolla (2003) showed that compared with Anglo voters, Latinos' partisanship is more influenced by observable political factors due to not having a long history of partisan socialization. García (2016) showed that across generations of Latinos, a group-based affinity is bonded by a shared "community of culture" and "community of interests." Kuo, Malhotra, and Mo (2014) found that exposure to microaggressive comments leads to more significant support for the Democratic Party among Asian Americans. At a minimum, simply not being anti-immigration would be necessary to attract this group to a political party.

Research on second-generation Americans shows that they more often grew up in a nonpolitical household (see Hajnal and Lee 2011). Their parents, by definition, are first-generation immigrants, and they are not themselves tied into long-standing political socialization processes whereby they are deeply connected to a particular party or the nation in general. Because party identification is one of those foundational concepts that political science has shown is preeminent in understanding voting behavior and attitudes toward policy, the lack of association with a political party for second-generation Americans means that it is plausible that they are still in flux and potentially persuadable about which parties to support and about attitudes toward the United States in general. In sum, this literature shows that lemma 3 is supported and that there exists the potential for change for second-generation Americans.

Lemma 4: Lack of Intent in Trump's Rhetoric in 2016

I now lay out the reasons why we might suspect that Trump had no intention of preventing or dissuading second-generation Americans from incorporating into America and the Republican Party. This is the most difficult of the four lemmas to test because it is impossible to actually measure Trump's intention. All that is possible is to measure expressed intention and make basic assumptions about rational behavior, which may or may not be applicable in Trump's case. When looking at his actual expressed desires and what would be rational for an electoral candidate, there is no reason to suspect that he desired his rhetoric to have a negative impact on second-generation Americans. Below, I show support for the fact that he derives no benefit or gain by alienating second-generation Americans from the nation in general or the Republican Party specifically and expressed no desire for this either.

Starting with expressed intention, Trump's rhetoric has never explicitly indicated immigrants' actual desire to incorporate less into America. He has said several times that a chief problem with immigrants is that they do not incorporate, assimilate, or otherwise become part of American society. For example, in a speech on May 19, 2019, Trump said his optimal plan for future immigration would "promote integration, assimilation, and national unity" and emphasized that "future immigrants will be required to learn English and to pass a civics exam prior to admission" (Trump 2019). The clear implication of this statement is that he wants immigrant families to integrate, assimilate, promote national unity, and so forth. Thus, Trump's expressed rhetoric is not, in fact, anti-incorporation, even if it is anti-immigration.

This fear over the lack of assimilation of immigrants is widespread among the base of the Republican Party. It is commonly mentioned as one of the chief reasons modern immigration—especially immigration from Mexico—is harmful (see, e.g., Huntington 2004). Because of this worry over the lack of assimilation, preventing immigrants' assimilation is probably not Trump's goal if one takes his words at face value. Thus, by measuring Trump's expressed intention, there is no evidence that inhibiting second-generation Americans' incorporation has been one of his goals.

Now turning toward analyzing basic assumptions about electoral candidates' rational behavior, we can see no benefit from Trump alienating second-generation Americans from the Republican Party. The clustering of second-generation Americans in battleground states is extremely important because the Electoral College is biased toward a few states. Presidential elections in the United States are often decided by a relatively small number of voters clustered in a few battleground states. Since voting patterns in these states have been well established for decades, it is unlikely that a massive switch in voting will occur among individuals from families with long-term partisan identifications. State-level partisan realignments do happen, but they are rare in American politics. The main chance for political parties to dramatically increase their share of the electorate will be by developing long-term partisan identification within recent immigrant groups.

The 2020 presidential election shows an increase in Latino voting for Trump in Florida and Texas, but data on second-generation Latinos or other ethnic groups does not show this shift (see chapter 7). We know that many states have been decided by 1 percentage point in two of the last three presidential elections. Up to 20% of some state populations are foreign-born (US Census Bureau 2017). Due to the large relative size of the state's second-generation American population, a shift in its partisan identification and subsequent vote choice for president could flip a battleground state to being solidly Democratic.

A simple mathematical exercise for Florida can illustrate the profound importance of second-generation Americans' estrangement from the Republican Party. The chief battleground state for the last 20 years has been Florida. The 29 Electoral College votes associated with Florida could easily be enough to ensure Democratic victory in a presidential election. Note that Florida has very close races in other statewide elections, such as senatorial and gubernatorial elections. Thus, a profound shift in second-generation Americans' partisan attachment due to Trump's anti-immigration rhetoric could do lasting damage to the Republican Party. Around 20% of Florida residents are immigrants, and they have a higher birth rate than Americans born in the country (US Census Bureau 2017). So, it may be assumed that at least 20% of Florida's electorate will be second-generation Americans in the near future. Only a single percentage point has decided Florida in several recent elections. Suppose we see an 11 percentage point decline in support for the Republican Party due to this rhetoric (which I show below), and party identification correlates at around 90 percentage points with actual voting behavior. In that case, we can expect about a 2 percentage point shift in the state voting: 20% of state population × 11% change in party ID due to rhetoric × 90% correlation between party ID and voting = 1.98% total vote shift (0.2 × 0.11 × 0.9 = 0.0198). Of course, this is not assured as many of the immigrants to South Florida, for example, are very wealthy elites from South America who are already conservative and this complicates the argument that second-generation Americans could shift the results in some states in the future, as is shown in chapter 7's results for Cuban Americans. But this margin is greater than that for four of Florida's last six presidential elections if this happens.

Considering that party identification lasts a lifetime for most voters, the impact of anti-immigration rhetoric on party identification of second-generation Americans could shift the results in many states and determine future presidential elections' outcomes. Nevada, for example, is sometimes won in statewide elections by Republicans, and it has a large population of second-generation Americans. The next tier of battleground states also has enough second-generation Americans to flip the states to being solidly Democratic if the voting patterns reflect a profound change. For example, North Carolina and Georgia have enough second-generation Americans to influence these states' election outcomes potentially. Even in battleground states that do not have large immigrant populations, such as Ohio, second-generation Americans still can sway election results because extremely close margins often decide these states. Thus, it is not in the interest of the Republican Party or its candidates to alienate these voters.

In sum, both the expressed intention and the rational behavior expectations of electoral candidates predict that Trump was not actually trying to alienate this group from America broadly or the Republican Party specifically. There is no other evidence that would suggest that this was a goal, and both the expressed intention and rational behavior of electoral candidates suggest that it is not an intended outcome of Trump's anti-immigration rhetoric.

Conclusion

This chapter established that Trump's rhetoric was unique and that its impact was potentially meaningful. Since I have established that the media covered Trump on the topic of immigration, and that his rhetoric was much more negative than prior presidents and that immigrants' children feel much more afraid of and angry toward him, it is plausible that second-generation Americans will internalize that frustration and may apply it to the United States generally or the Republican Party specifically.

I established this impact by examining how Trump's rhetoric was covered in the media compared with prior presidents or candidates. I also compared how immigrants felt about him as a nominee versus their feelings about prior presidential candidates. Trump was found to be more hostile toward immigration and more focused on the negatives of immigration. He was also noted to provoke more negative affect from the children of immigrants. However, the survey methodology cannot establish anything more than correlation. To delve into the causal mechanisms, we need experimental research whereby causation can be fully established. Understanding the outcomes of this novel, divisive rhetoric is crucial. Trump's use of anti-immigration themes was consistent and extended far beyond the campaign and throughout his presidency.

Survey research is valuable in that it allows a broad-based sample. Furthermore, the ANES data allow an estimate of how the attitudes of second-generation Americans have changed over time. Good research aims for both external and internal validity, and it is essential to show that the effect is a valid finding outside of the artificial, contrived setting of experiments where complete causal control is possible by using real-world data as in this chapter.

Of course, there is the possibility that second-generation Americans may forget about the anti-immigrant rhetoric in future elections and that my research only tests the current state of public opinion. There is the possibility that Republicans (or Democrats) could create a new enemy for future elections, and immigration may not be the focus, which may not impact second-generation immigrant voters as much. Also, multiple alternative explanations may exist for why second-generation Americans dislike Trump or are afraid of him, such as his personality, his treatment of women, his attitude toward trade, and so on. My intent in the empirical chapters is to show causality. The data will show that Trump's specific rhetoric lowers second-generation Americans' willingness to incorporate into the broader American sphere, and it also lowers their opinion of Trump and the Republican Party.

To test this impact, I conduct survey experiments where real rhetoric from Donald Trump is read by second-generation Americans and then the impact of reading this rhetoric is measured. The chief difference between Trump and his predecessors relies on how immigrants were talked about in the 2016 election. That is the direct test of that recent anti-immigration rhetoric, but these findings are augmented in this chapter by examining nationally representative survey data over time on this topic. An optimal social science methodology is a multimethod approach whereby each method's potential pros and cons are augmented by the pros and cons of the other methods. Showing the effect across multiple methods bolsters our confidence in the validity of the findings.

I will test the potential implications of this theoretical model in the subsequent chapters with both experimental and survey research. The research shows that Trump's rhetoric has a nonminimal effect on this population, as predicted by this model. Exposure to Trump's rhetoric leads to a decrease in attachment to American identity patriotism and support for the Republican Party. This research uses experimental, aggregate, and survey data to test the anti-immigration rhetoric's impact on second-generation Americans.

References

Altemeyer, Bob. 1981. *Right-Wing Authoritarianism*. Winnipeg: University of Manitoba Press.

Alvarez, R. Michael, and L. García Bedolla. 2003. "The Foundations of Latino Voter Partisanship: Evidence from the 2000 Elections." *Journal of Politics* 65 (1): 31–49.

Converse, Phillip E. 1964. "The Nature of Belief Systems in Mass Publics." In *Ideology and Discontent*, edited by David E. Apter. New York: Free Press of Glencoe.

Emerson, Rupert. 1960. *From Empire to Nation*. Boston: Beacon Press.

García, John A. 2016. *Latino Politics in America: Community, Culture, and Interests*. New York: Rowman and Littlefield.

Hajnal, Zoltan, and Taeku Lee. 2011. *Why Americans Don't Join the Party: Race, Immigration, and the Failure (of Political Parties) to Engage the Electorate*. Princeton: Princeton University Press.

Huntington, Samuel. 2004. *Who Are We? The Challenges to America's National Identity*. New York: Simon & Shuster.

Jennings, M. Kent, and Richard G. Niemi. 1968. "The Transmission of Political Values from Parent to Child." *American Political Science Review* 62 (2): 169–84.

Kuo, Alexander, Neil A. Malhotra, and Cecilia Mo. 2014. "Why Do Asian Americans Identify as Democrats? Testing Theories of Social Exclusion and Intergroup Solidarity." February 25. Available at SSRN: http://dx.doi.org/10.2139/ssrn.2423950

Lazarsfeld, Paul Felix, Bernard Berelson, and Hazel Gaudet. 1944. *The People's Choice: How the Voter Makes Up His Mind in a Presidential Campaign*. New York: Columbia University Press.

Macnamara, Jim. 2005. "Media Content Analysis: Its Uses, Benefits and Best Practice Methodology." *Asia Pacific Public Relations Journal* 6 (1): 1–34.

Neuendorf, Kimberly A. 2002. *The Content Analysis Guidebook*. Thousand Oaks, CA: Sage.

Pantoja, Adrian D., Ricardo Ramírez, and Gary M. Segura. 2001. "Citizens by Choice, Voters by Necessity: Patterns in Political Mobilization by Naturalized Latinos." *Political Research Quarterly* 54:729–50.

Ramakrishnan, S. Karthick. 2005. *Democracy in Immigrant America: Changing Demographics and Political Participation*. Palo Alto, CA: Stanford University Press.

Ramakrishnan, S. Karthick, and Thomas J. Espenshade. 2001. "Immigrant Incorporation and Political Participation in the United States." *International Migration Review* 35 (3): 870–909.

Sears, David O., and Carolyn Funk. 1999. "Evidence of the Long-Term Persistence of Adults' Political Predispositions." *Journal of Politics* 61 (1): 1–28.

Sears, David O., and Nicholas A. Valentino. 1997. "Politics Matters: Political Events as Catalysts for Preadult Socialization." *American Political Science Review* 91 (1): 45–65.

Stenner, Karen. 2005. *The Authoritarian Dynamic*. Cambridge: Cambridge University Press.

Stryker, J. E., R. J. Wray, R. C. Hornik, and I. Yanovitzky. 2006. "Validation of Database Search Terms for Content Analysis: The Case of Cancer News Coverage." *Journalism & Mass Communication Quarterly* 83 (2): 413–30.

Trump, Donald. 2019. "Remarks by President Trump on Modernizing Our Immigration System for a Stronger America" (Speech). May 16. https://www.whitehouse.gov/briefings-statements/remarks-president-trump-modernizing-immigration-system-stronger-america/

US Census Bureau. 2017. "Selected Housing Characteristics, 2010–2015 American Community Survey 5-Year Estimates." http://factfinder2.census.gov/faces/tableservices/jsf/pages/productview.xhtml?pid=ACS_11_5YR_DP04

Weber, R. 1990. *Basic Content Analysis*. 2nd ed. Newbury Park, CA: Sage.

Wong, Janelle. 2000. "The Effects of Age and Political Exposure on the Development of Party Identification among Asian American and Latino Immigrants in the United States." *Political Behavior* 22 (4): 341–71.

CHAPTER 4

Trump Rhetorical Analysis

This book has presented Trump's rhetoric as anti-immigration, but I have not yet provided evidence to support this claim. In this chapter, I detail Trump's rhetoric and cite specific examples that are clearly anti-immigration. I also show that he is disproportionately concerned with immigration compared with prior presidents. More formally, I use sentiment analysis to detail the degree to which his rhetoric is anti-immigration. Finally, I show how this anti-immigration rhetoric allowed him to obtain the nomination in 2016 by providing him a route to power.

The United States is often described as a land of immigrants, but each immigration wave created a considerable backlash that provided electoral incentives for some politicians to bash immigrants. Further, the motivation to become a politician could be stimulated in individuals holding deeply anti-immigrant beliefs in an era of high immigration. In combination, these forces have produced a long history of anti-immigration rhetoric from politicians in the United States. From Benjamin Franklin to the present day, making negative comments about immigration has been common and often used as a pathway to political power. Whether these comments were derived from legitimate concerns over potential problems created by immigration or were merely pandering to anti-immigrant sentiment within the population is hard to discern. However, such rhetoric has been almost constant in any period in American history that featured a large wave of immigration.

Immigration has especially been at the forefront of American politics since 2000, when the US Census showed that Hispanics had become the second-largest racial or ethnic group, while immigration from Asia was also significantly on the rise. Based on prior history, the predictable outcome was that anti-immigration rhetoric from politicians would follow. This rhetoric was further enabled by the rise of partisan media during the same period, which amplified those who opposed immigration. Increased immigration was occurring concurrently with globalization that produced variable economic gains and losses for different areas of the country. These conditions provided fertile soil for nationalistic populism to grow in the United States. The rise of Donald Trump happened against this backdrop.

I start by showing specific examples of Trump's rhetoric that are clearly anti-immigration. This rhetoric's scope and intensity show the need to study its potential impact on the children of immigrants.

Specific Examples of Trump's Anti-Immigration Rhetoric

Research has shown that how elites discuss immigrants affects attitudes toward them (Boomgaarden and Vliegenthart 2009). This circumstance is especially true of immigrant or minority groups for which the majority population may not have day-to-day familiarity in social relations and may only know through media representations (Baker, Gabrielatos, and McEnery 2013). To dig deeper into precisely what Trump has said about immigration, I present examples of his rhetoric that clearly show that his anti-immigration statements are not merely a minor part of his discourse but have played a significant role in the daily news cycle in the United States since 2015.

Trump began his campaign by giving a campaign announcement speech in which he stated, "When Mexico sends its people, they're not sending their best. They're not sending you. They're not sending you. They're sending people that have lots of problems and they're bringing those problems with us. They're bringing drugs, they're bringing crime, they're rapists, and some, I assume, are good people" (Time Staff 2015). On July 5, 2015, Trump defended making these comments by saying, "The Mexican government is forcing their most unwanted people into the United States. They are, in many cases, criminals, drug dealers, rapists, etc. This was evident just this week when, as an example, a young woman in San Francisco was viciously killed by a five-time deported Mexican with a long criminal record who was forced back into the United States because they didn't want him in Mexico. This is merely one of thousands of similar incidents throughout the United States" (Walker 2015). These are clearly anti-immigrantion statements that may affect the views of the children of immigrants.

The central question asked in the remainder of the book is whether it is possible to listen to statements like these if your parents are from Mexico and not think differently of the United States or the Republican Party. Importantly, these statements continued beyond Trump's campaign, extending throughout his presidency. For example, Trump wrote on Twitter on May 16, 2018, "We have people coming into the country or trying to come in, we're stopping a lot of them, but we're taking people out of the country. You wouldn't believe how bad these people are." He continued by tweeting, "These aren't people. These are animals." Most people would deem referring to other humans as "animals" to be harsh rhetoric. To relate to the theory stated in chapter 2, the size of the stimulus concerning prior norms of discourse is large and unique for a sitting president; therefore, it could be impactful in ways that prior less-inflammatory rhetoric was not.

To display more specific examples of Trump's rhetoric about immigration, table 2 shows a selection of immigration tweets. The table focuses on Twitter because this platform is one of the primary ways that Trump communicated when he was president, and his tweets were often the subject of subsequent news articles.

These tweets clearly show that Trump's rhetoric is against immigration, and the rhetoric that he uses to describe it is often harsh. Additionally, the sheer number of subtopics that Trump discusses when speaking about immigration is staggering. Using data from politifact.com, I compiled the following list of campaign promises given by Trump concerning immigration.[1]

Remove all undocumented immigrants—"We have at least 11 million people in this country that came in illegally. They will go out. They will come back—some will come back, the best, through a process. They have to come back legally. They have to come back through a process, and it may not be a very quick process, but I think that's very fair, and very fine."

Cancel all funding of sanctuary cities—"We will end the sanctuary cities that have resulted in so many needless deaths. Cities that refuse to cooperate with federal authorities will not receive taxpayer dollars, and we will work with Congress to pass legislation to protect those jurisdictions that do assist federal authorities."

---

1. This list of campaign rhetoric and titles listed for each type of rhetoric was taken from https://www.politifact.com/truth-o-meter/promises/trumpometer/subjects/immigration/

TABLE 2. Selected Tweets about Immigration by Donald Trump

Date	Text of Tweet by Donald Trump
June 30, 2015	"We MUST have strong borders and stop illegal immigration. Without that we do not have a country. Also, Mexico is killing U.S. on trade. WIN!"
July 1, 2015	"For all of those who want to #MakeAmericaGreatAgain, boycott @Macys. They are weak on border security & stopping illegal immigration."
July 11, 2015	"Legal immigrants want border security. It is common sense. We must build a wall! Let's Make America Great Again!"
August 22, 2015	"Now that I started my war on illegal immigration and securing the border, most other candidates are finally speaking up. Just politicians!"
August 26, 2016	"I am very proud to have brought the subject of illegal immigration back into the discussion. Such a big problem for our country-I will solve"
February 12, 2016	"I will end illegal immigration and protect our borders! We need to MAKE AMERICA SAFE & GREAT AGAIN! #Trump2016"
June 24, 2018	"We cannot allow all of these people to invade our Country. When somebody comes in, we must immediately, with no Judges or Court Cases, bring them back from where they came. Our system is a mockery to good immigration policy and Law and Order. Most children come without parents . . ."
October 29, 2018	"Many Gang Members and some very bad people are mixed into the Caravan heading to our Southern Border. Please go back, you will not be admitted into the United States unless you go through the legal process."
October 29, 2018	"This is an invasion of our Country and our Military is waiting for you!"
November 18, 2018	"The U.S. is ill-prepared for this invasion, and will not stand for it. [Migrants] are causing crime and big problems in Mexico. Go home!"
January 11, 2019	"I just got back [from the southern border] and it is a far worse situation than almost anyone would understand, an invasion!"
January 31, 2019	"More troops being sent to the Southern Border to stop the attempted invasion of Illegals, through large Caravans, into our Country."
June 2, 2019	"People have been saying for years that we should talk to Mexico. The problem is that Mexico is an 'abuser' of the United States, taking but never giving. It has been this way for decades. Either they stop the invasion of our Country by Drug Dealers, Cartels, Human Traffickers . . ."
	"Coyotes and Illegal Immigrants, which they can do very easily, or our many companies and jobs that have been foolishly allowed to move South of the Border, will be brought back into the United States through taxation (Tariffs). America has had enough!"

Build a wall, and make Mexico pay for it—"I would build a great wall, and nobody builds walls better than me, believe me, and I'll build them very inexpensively. I will build a great great wall on our southern border and I'll have Mexico pay for that wall."

Establish a ban on Muslims entering the U.S.—"Donald J. Trump is calling for a total and complete shutdown of Muslims entering the United States until our country's representatives can figure out what the hell is going on."

Suspend immigration from terror-prone places—"And if people don't like it, we've got to have a country folks. Got to have a country. Countries in which immigration will be suspended would include places like Syria and Libya. And we are going to stop the tens of thousands of people coming in from Syria."

Limit legal immigration—"We will reform legal immigration to serve the best interests of America and its workers, the forgotten people. Workers. We're going to take care of our workers."

Have mandatory minimum sentences for criminals caught trying to enter the United States illegally—"On my first day in office, I am also going to ask Congress to pass 'Kate's Law'—named for Kate Steinle—to ensure that criminal aliens convicted of illegal re-entry receive strong mandatory minimum sentences."

Remove existing Syrian refugees—"I'm putting the people on notice that are coming here from Syria, as part of this mass migration, that if I win, if I win, they're going back."

Ending birthright citizenship—"End birthright citizenship."

Increasing visa fees—"Increase fees on all border crossing cards—of which we issue about 1 million to Mexican nationals each year (a major source of visa overstays)."

Hire American workers first—"Establish new immigration controls to boost wages and to ensure that open jobs are offered to American workers first."

Replace J-1 Visa with Inner City Resume Bank—"The J-1 visa jobs program for foreign youth will be terminated and replaced with a resume bank for inner city youth provided to all corporate subscribers to the J-1 visa program."

Triple ICE enforcement—"We will triple the number of ICE agents."

Cancel visas to foreign countries that won't take undocumented immigrants back—"Cancel visas to foreign countries that won't take them back."

Terminate Barack Obama's immigration executive orders "immediately"—"Immediately terminate President Obama's two illegal executive amnesties (Deferred Action for Parents of Americans and Lawful Permanent Residents and Deferred Action for Childhood Arrivals). All immigration laws will be enforced—we will triple the number of ICE agents. Anyone who enters the U.S. illegally is subject to deportation. That is what it means to have laws and to have a country."

The extensive breadth of topics is significant because, besides being hostile rhetoric, another component of my theory is that it was broadcast so widely that second-generation Americans would almost certainly have been exposed to it. An essential part of that exposure is that it was long term as well as widespread. If the exposure had been broad but only short term, second-generation Americans could have tuned out the news cycle during the brief period that the rhetoric was broadcast. By showing Trump's long-term use of anti-immigration rhetoric embedded in many topics, I show that most second-generation Americans were almost certainly exposed to his rhetoric at some point.

So far, the analysis in this chapter has been purely subjective, but now I turn to an objective approach to show that Trump's rhetoric is, in fact, hostile toward immigration.

Sentiment Analysis of Trump's Rhetoric

One approach for determining whether Trump's rhetoric is actually anti-immigrant is to use quantitative text analysis techniques to evaluate a large batch of his tweets. I scraped every tweet from March 2011 to March 2020 posted by Trump and selected those with the word "immigration." This process led to a universe of 313 tweets. A reading of these tweets suggests that they were highly anti-immigrant. However, such subjective interpretations could be biased.

To alleviate this concern, I turned to a machine learning technique called sentiment analysis.[2] Quantitative text analysis uses software to quan-

---

2. Specifically, I used the sentimentr package in R to analyze this section.

tify text (Hopkins and King 2010), and sentiment analysis has been shown to accurately and objectively code text as positive or negative (Taboada et al. 2011). Researchers create a dictionary that rates every word in the English language on a scale from −2 to +2 based on how negative or positive it is, respectively. The validity of sentiment analysis has been shown by researchers who compared intercoder reliability between hypothesis blind coders and the software's interpretation of a text (Kiritchenko, Zhu, and Mohammad 2014). The sentiment analysis derived through quantitative text analysis is typically highly correlated with human coders' subjective interpretations (Grimmer and Stewart 2013).

Once this validity was established, a rapid expansion occurred in research using sentiment analysis to assess whether social media posts and tweets were positive or negative (see, e.g., Haselmayer and Jenny 2017; Martínez-Cámara et al. 2014). Importantly, research has validated sentiment analysis using Twitter and real-world data, such as the stock market (see Bollen, Mao, and Zeng 2011). This mechanistic approach to quantitative text analysis is a helpful check on subjective interpretations. The results based on this method align with a subjective understanding of how Trump talks about immigration, but they also ensure that the analysis of his rhetoric is empirically valid. This validation is important because negative feelings toward Trump for reasons other than his rhetoric could color or bias the interpretation of that rhetoric. Machine learning, however, undertakes sentiment analysis without bias.

Table 3 shows the results of the sentiment analysis of Trump's immigration tweets. Based on the lexicon used in this analysis, Trump's tweets about immigration are negative. The median and mean sentiment are less than 0, which signifies that the majority of words used in these tweets are negative, which implies that the tweets' sentiment is negative. This unsupervised approach quantitatively establishes that Trump's rhetoric is anti-immigration, as the 313 tweets that mentioned immigration are, on average, negative. Sentiment analysis is difficult to interpret directly. This difficulty is because this metric is derived from counting every word automatically, and human language can contain both positive and negative words, even if the sentence's meaning is negative. For example, Trump tweeted on Febru-

TABLE 3. Sentiment Analysis of Trump's Immigration Tweets

Min	1st Quarter	Median	Mean	3rd Quarter	Max.
−1.278	−0.190	−0.017	−0.035	0.116	0.879

ary 11, 2017, "Our legal system is broken! '77% of refugees allowed into U.S. since travel reprieve hail from seven suspect countries.' (WT) SO DANGEROUS!" The words "allowed," "reprieve," and "hail" are all considered positive by the model, even though this tweet is clearly negative. So a direct interpretation of the distribution is not informative, and the means are the best metric for sentiment analysis. Although not perfect, sentiment analysis still provides one metric in combination with the other evidence that I provided in the chapter that shows empirically that Trump's rhetoric is, in fact, anti-immigrant.

Presenting a more fine-grained analysis, figure 10 shows a histogram of the distribution of the coding of the words in these tweets. Although some words were coded as positive, the histogram's overall shape skews to the negative side. It is important to remember that many of Trump's tweets conveyed multiple messages. For example, he often tweeted, "Win!" That word was coded as a positive sentiment, but it was not positive about immigration in the context of the tweet; instead, it referred to his presidential campaign. The mechanistic approach of quantitative text analysis cannot discern such fine distinctions, so one must use caution in interpreting the results. Where quantitative text analysis works best is as a check on potentially biased readings of the text. In sum, the majority of sentiments expressed in Trump's tweets about immigration are negative.

How does Trump compare with past presidents about immigration rhetoric? To answer this question, it is necessary to assess speeches that previous presidents have given. No president other than Obama has ever used Twitter as a communication mechanism while in office, and speeches have historically been the main form of presidential communication. To make a comparison between Trump's rhetoric and that of past presidents, I focused on official presidential speeches. I used a corpus of all presidential speeches up to Obama[3] and then I added speeches from Trump.[4]

Table 4 shows the results based on a word-presence technique, which simply counts whether a speech mentions immigration or immigrants. This value is a measure of focus; I have already shown that Trump's sentiment toward immigration is negative in his tweeting, and any reading of his speeches shows that he is undoubtedly negative about immigration for

---

3. This corpus is from Brown (2016). This is described as a collection of presidential speeches that were officially given while in office. It was selected because it had a large number of speeches from presidents.

4. The text of the Trump speeches was taken from https://millercenter.org/the-presidency/presidential-speeches?field_president_target_id[8396]=8396

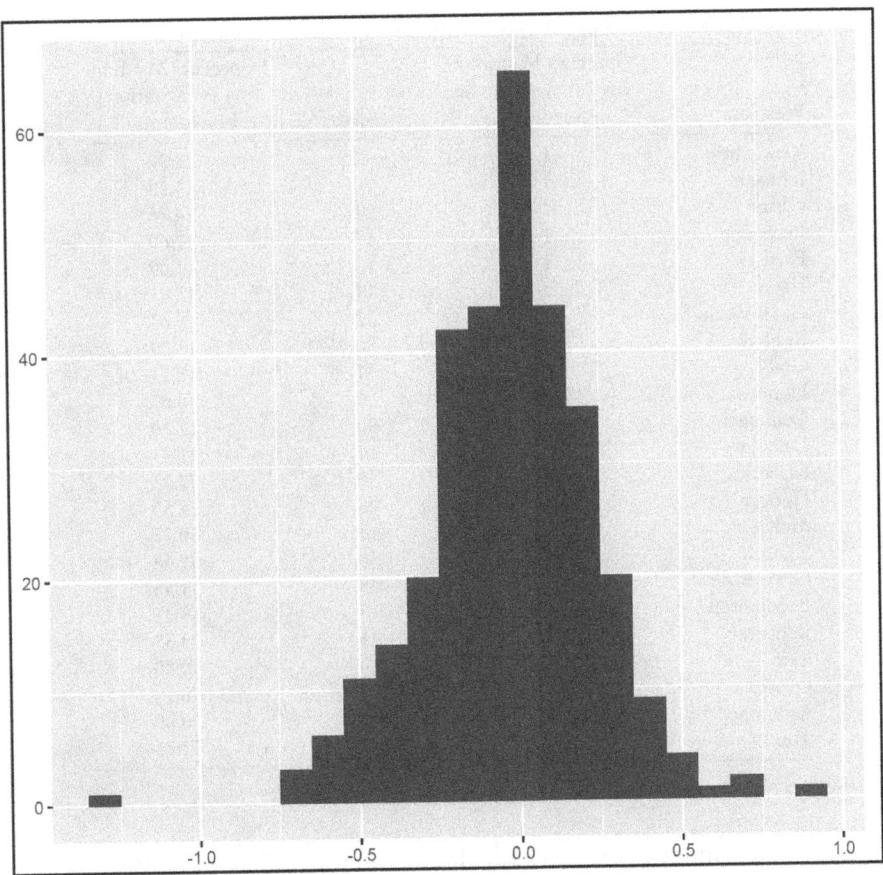

Fig. 10. Results of the sentiment analysis for Trump's immigration tweets.

the United States. What is comparable across presidencies is the amount of attention that a particular president gives to immigration. Every president that mentioned immigration or immigrants in an official speech is listed in table 4. If a president is not listed, then he did not mention immigration or immigrants in a speech. Table 3 also shows the total number of speeches that a president made and the percentage that included mention of immigration or immigrants.

Table 4 clearly shows that Trump is the only president who focused on immigration in most of his speeches. Interestingly, Obama is closely related in terms of percentage to Trump, reflecting the importance of immigration in this era. However, Trump focused the most on immigration, and second-

TABLE 4. Presidential Speeches Mentioning Immigration or Immigrants

President	Speeches Mentioning Immigration or Immigrants (N)	Speeches (N)	Speeches Mentioning Immigration or Immigrants (%)
Kennedy	1	44	2.27
Johnson	3	70	4.28
Carter	1	21	4.76
Buchanan	1	13	7.69
Ford	1	13	7.69
Hayes	2	15	13.33
G. H. W. Bush	3	22	13.64
Reagan	8	58	13.79
Grant	5	31	16.13
Filmore	1	6	16.67
Coolidge	7	40	17.50
Lincoln	3	14	21.43
Cleveland	7	30	23.33
Hoover	8	28	28.57
McKinley	4	13	30.77
Clinton	12	38	31.58
G. W. Bush	12	38	31.58
B. Harrison	5	15	33.33
Roosevelt	7	21	33.33
Taft	4	10	40.00
Obama	24	49	48.10
Arthur	5	11	50.00
Trump	16	22	72.72

generation Americans would easily have been exposed to his rhetoric during this period due to his frequent mention of the topic.

Now that it is established that Trump's rhetoric is anti-immigration and that he has given the most speeches about immigration of any president, the following section examines the influence of Trump's anti-immigration rhetoric on the 2016 Republican presidential primaries' electoral outcome.

The Role of Anti-Immigration Rhetoric in Trump's Rise

Anti-immigration rhetoric was vital to Trump's rise in the presidential primary of 2016. Trump was polling poorly in the Republican Party presidential primary until he started attacking immigration. The first speech in which he attacked immigration was on June 16, 2015. This speech contained his announcement that he was launching his campaign for the Republican nomination for the presidency. Immediately after his campaign announcement, he rose sharply in the polls. Before this speech, he was polling around 3% in national polls, but afterward, his support immediately increased by 8 percentage points to 11.5%. Further, on July 5, he gave a lengthy, pointed rebuttal to people who had criticized the anti-immigration statements in his campaign announcement speech. This rebuttal garnered extensive press coverage and featured even harsher rhetoric about immigration.

Figure 11 shows Republican polling[5] for Trump from 2015 through the date that he attained the nomination in May 2016. Additionally, it shows that the speeches on June 16 and July 5 led to a significant increase in support for his nomination. Of course, any campaign announcement will drive attention to the candidate, and it is not possible to discern whether the anti-immigration rhetoric, in particular, led to a jump in approval for Trump. Also, note that the campaign announcement speech touched on many other topics, including his stance against free trade with China and Mexico, which was a position that was popular with the public.

The July 5 statement allows a more precise examination of the impact of anti-immigration statements because that statement was solely on the topic of immigration. Immediately afterward, Trump experienced a jump of around 5 percentage points in the national polling. Although it is difficult to ascertain exact causal relationships in an incredibly complicated and multifaceted primary campaign environment, these results are certainly suggestive that Trump's path to power was facilitated by anti-immigration rhetoric.

In 2012, Trump expressed very little anti-immigration rhetoric, as he primarily focused on promoting conspiracies about Barack Obama's birth certificate and the topic of vaccinations. The nativist rhetoric was a new topic for Trump in the 2016 campaign. What is interesting is how this talk helped him in the primary season. Before he started bashing immigrants, he was polling around 2% to 3% in national election surveys. Afterward, he quickly ascended to the polls' leading position, gaining around 12 to 15 percentage points. After that, he never relinquished the lead, except for a brief period when Ben Carson replaced him. Of note, Carson became the leader once he started publicly speaking against political correctness.

Carson's surge in the polls raises another potential impact of Trump's rhetoric that cannot be discerned in this research; however, it may provide an avenue of study for future researchers. The popularity of Trump's rheto-

---

5. This table uses polling data collected by the website FiveThirtyEight. See https://projects.fivethirtyeight.com/election-2016/national-primary-polls/republican/

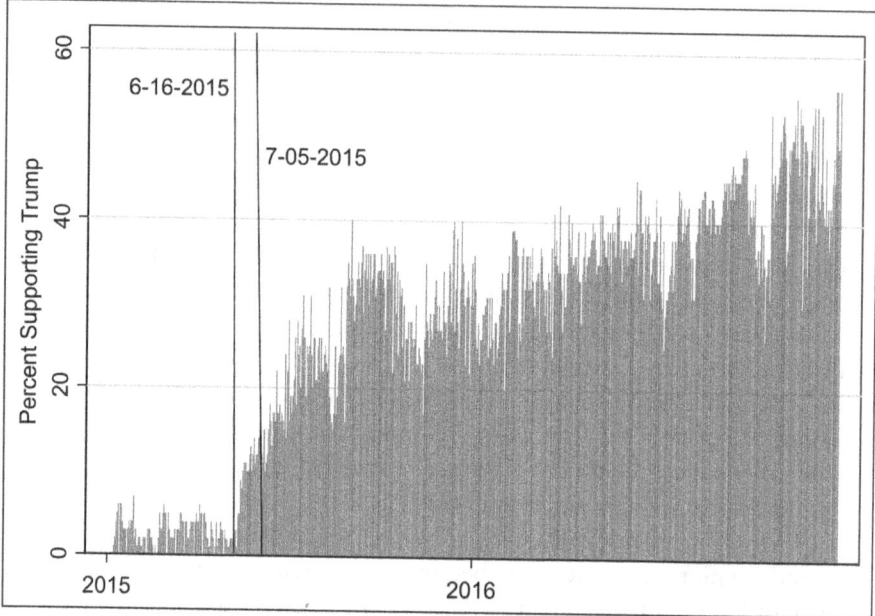

Fig. 11. Polling support for Trump in the Republican primary in 2015 and 2016 and the dates of two major anti-immigration speeches.

ric may have derived from anti-immigrant feelings, but another possibility is that his stance against political correctness attracted the Republican primary electorate. The mere fact that Trump was willing to strongly violate norms of discourse and thereby show his political incorrectness could have attracted primary voters. This possibility does not negate the zeal for anti-immigration rhetoric among Republican primary voters, but it could augment its appeal. A combination of a desire to hear a politician violate the norms of political correctness and approval of his view of immigration, which many other Republicans were not addressing, may have caught the interest of Republican primary voters. Until Trump's rise, the Republican primary featured politicians such as Jeb Bush and Marco Rubio, who were more moderate on immigration and certainly more moderate in their rhetoric about it.

Conclusion

This review of the evidence shows that Trump's rhetoric was indeed anti-immigration. Compared with previous presidents, Trump centered his rhetoric more heavily on immigration, and the sentiment analysis showed that it almost exclusively portrayed immigration in a negative light. I showed empirically that this rhetoric was against immigration and hostile toward immigrants from the beginning of his campaign in 2015 up to tweets in early 2021. By the end of Trump's first term, an entire six-year period of his anti-immigration rhetoric will have dominated the news cycle in American politics. Empirical research on the potential outcomes of this type of rhetoric is clearly needed. As we have seen, even at the height of the most anti-immigrant periods in US history, prior presidents did not speak of immigration as often as Trump does now. For example, less than 20% of Calvin Coolidge's speeches in the 1920s—a period of intense anti-immigrant feelings—included mention of immigrants or immigration. Trump's anti-immigration rhetoric, appearing in more than 72% of his speeches, is historically distinct and therefore essential to study.

This review of Trump's actual rhetoric shows that he is not only hostile toward immigration but goes far beyond the traditional critiques of immigration in public policy literature. Many scholars have noted possible negative aspects of immigration, such as its impact on low-wage employment or its potential burden on rural areas' social services. I showed that Trump's rhetoric does not invoke these traditional concerns and certainly does not invoke them in a traditional manner. His rhetoric is focused on high-salience, adverse outcomes that are more conspiratorial than fact-based. For example, his often-repeated claim that immigrants commit large amounts of crime is not supported by criminology research (Light, He, and Robey 2020). His rhetoric might be best described as fear-mongering, and it panders to individuals who already hold a negative view of immigrants. Also shown in this chapter is how beneficial Trump's anti-immigration rhetoric was to his 2016 presidential campaign.

In conclusion, this chapter shows that Trump was something new in American politics and his anti-immigration rhetoric requires study. We currently have a large wave of immigrants in the United States, and their children are just now navigating the American political world. The impact of Trump's rhetoric on their political participation is crucial to investigate empirically, which I begin to do with experiments in the next chapter.

References

Baker, Paul, Costas Gabrielatos, and Tony McEnery. 2013. *Discourse Analysis and Media Attitudes: The Representation of Islam in the British Press.* Cambridge: Cambridge University Press.

Bollen, Johan, Huina Mao, and Xiao-Jun Zeng. 2011. "Twitter Mood Predicts the Stock Market." *Journal of Computational Science* 2 (1): 1–8.
Boomgaarden, Hajo G., and Rens Vliegenthart. 2009. "How News Content Influences Anti-Immigration Attitudes: Germany, 1993–2005." *European Journal of Political Research* 48 (4): 516–42.
Brown, David W. 2016. Corpus of Presidential Speeches. http://www.thegrammarlab.com
Grimmer, Justin, and Brandon M. Stewart. 2013. "Text as Data: The Promise and Pitfalls of Automated Content Analysis Methods for Political Texts." *Political Analysis* 21 (3): 267–97.
Haselmayer, M., and M. Jenny. 2017. "Sentiment Analysis of Political Communication: Combining a Dictionary Approach with Crowdcoding." *Quality and Quantity* 51:2623–46.
Hopkins, Daniel, and Gary King. 2010. "A Method of Automated Nonparametric Content Analysis for Social Science." *American Journal of Political Science* 54 (1): 229–47.
Kiritchenko, Svetlana, Xiaodan Zhu, and Saif M. Mohammad. 2014. "Sentiment Analysis of Short Informal Texts." *Journal of Artificial Intelligence Research* 50:723–62.
Light, Michael T., Jingying He, and Jason P. Robey. 2020. "Comparing Crime Rates between Undocumented Immigrants, Legal Immigrants, and Native-Born US Citizens in Texas." *Proceedings of the National Academy of Sciences* 117 (51): 32340–47.
Martínez-Cámara, Eugenio, Maria Teresa Martín-Valdivia, Luis Alfonso Urena López, and Arturo Montejo Ráez. 2014. "Sentiment Analysis in Twitter." *Natural Language Engineering* 20 (1): 1–28.
Taboada, Maite, Julian Brooke, Milan Tofiloski, Kimberly Voll, and Manfred Stede. 2011. "Lexicon-Based Methods for Sentiment Analysis." *Computational Linguistics* 37 (2): 267–307.
Time Staff. 2015. "Here's Donald Trump's Presidential Announcement Speech." *Time*, June 16. https://time.com/3923128/donald-trump-announcement-speech/
Walker, Hunter. 2015. "Donald Trump Just Released an Epic Statement Raging against Mexican Immigrants and 'Disease.'" *Business Insider*, July 6. https://www.businessinsider.com/donald-trumps-epic-statement-on-mexico-2015-7

CHAPTER 5

Rhetoric and Attitudes toward America

The previous chapter showed the uniqueness and intensity of Trump's anti-immigration rhetoric, and I now examine how second-generation Americans react to this rhetoric. The impact of anti-immigration rhetoric on the second generation's feelings of American identity and patriotism[1] is unclear. Integrating the recent large wave of immigrants and their descendants is essential (Kasinitz, Mollenkopf, and Waters 2005). Understanding what helps or hinders their integration is crucial for social scientists (Alba and Nee 2003). In a period of intense anti-immigration rhetoric, assessing this rhetoric's impact on the ongoing integration process is necessary.

Research on the power of elite cues and the strong ties of identity suggests that anti-immigration rhetoric will be perceived as an attack on immigrants generally. In turn, it will be perceived as an attack on the social identity of second-generation Americans because it attacks their family, specifically their parents. Since many Americans nominated and voted for Trump and was perceived as the leader of the United States for four years, his hostile rhetoric may be construed as reflective of how Americans generally think.

Trump typically uses the phrase "illegal immigrants" and thereby does not directly or personally implicate second-generation Americans born in the United States. Even though Trump's rhetoric is not directly attacking these second-generation Americans since they are not undocumented, I still find a negative effect on their perceptions of America after they hear

---

[1]. Patriotism has almost exclusively been viewed as the love of and gratitude for one's nation. Huddy and Khatib (2007, 63) state that "there is broad agreement on the meaning of patriotism as 'a deeply felt affective attachment to the nation.'"

his rhetoric. This finding shows that second-generation Americans perceive elite cues directed against undocumented immigrants as a sign that America is less desirable to integrate into. Elite cues that bash undocumented immigrants may shape a heuristic for second-generation Americans, leading them to perceive that the United States is not a welcoming place and is, therefore, less desirable to incorporate into.

Specifically, using Trump's rhetoric in the 2016 US presidential election as a test case, I examined whether brief exposure to anti-immigration rhetoric reduced expressed patriotism and feeling of the importance of being an American. The online sample in this study had 500 adult US citizens with two foreign-born parents.[2] It was matched to nationally representative census data on demographics for second-generation Americans. Randomization produced balance across a large set of pretest variables (see appendix, table A1).

The results show a small but statistically significant negative effect of exposure to anti-immigrant discourse in lowering expressed patriotism and feelings of American identity among second-generation Americans. Although the rates of patriotism and American identity were high among second-generation Americans in all treatment conditions, the treatment group expressed less patriotism and felt that their American identity had less importance after exposure to Trump's anti-immigration rhetoric. Whether intentional or not, anti-immigration rhetoric alienated second-generation Americans. Consequently, Trump's anti-immigration rhetoric may exacerbate the potential problems he has complained about.

Census data show that 87% of children of immigrants are US citizens, with most having been born here. This second-generation lags in political participation (Mollenkopf and Hochschild 2010), and many scholars are worried about their political incorporation into the United States (Portes and Rumbaut 2001). Trump's rhetoric is not conducive to inspiring greater incorporation.

---

2. While there are competing definitions of second-generation citizens, following Ramakrishnan (2004), I am focusing on those Americans who have two foreign-born parents. The literature on second-generation Americans often defines them in this manner because having one native-born parent provides an essential set of parental socialization that is familiar with the American political parties and political systems. Those second-generation Americans who have both parents as foreign-born do not have access to a native-born parent and, therefore, will be less likely to have native socialization processes.

Elite Rhetoric Literature

There are two strands of relevant academic literature that discuss how elite discourse may affect public opinion through two mechanisms (Schneider and Jacoby 2005; however, see a counter perspective in Edwards 1996, 2003). The first mechanism is agenda-setting. As presidential discourse focuses on a topic, it increases public attention on it (Tulis 1988). It has been well established that the more a president speaks about a topic, the more attention the public gives the issue (Campbell and Jamieson 2008). For the most part, the press indexes its coverage of topics to those elites focus on (Bennett 1990; Bennett, Lawrence, and Livingston 2006). Further, elite rhetoric has been shown to influence natives' attitudes toward immigration (Ono and Sloop 2004), so it is plausible that it could also influence those of second-generation Americans.

The second mechanism is through cue taking or heuristics (Lupia 1994; Kernell 1997). If elites support an issue or express hostility toward specific groups, individuals who support those elites may be more likely to be influenced by the rhetoric (Popkin 1991; Lupia and McCubbins 1998). The elites are viewed as credible because they are trusted on other issues. When a new issue arises, their supporters take cues from them on how to respond. However, those who oppose the elites will take the opposite tack; they will view their reactions to new issues with skepticism because they distrust the elites.

In this case, we can expect supporters of Trump to become more opposed to illegal immigration and supporters of Hillary Clinton to become more supportive of immigrants when they heard that a Republican candidate advocated stricter immigration policies. My analysis of the 2016 ANES shows that 68% of Trump voters wanted to lower immigration rates, while only 24% of Clinton voters did. In general, heuristics are used in decision-making because we do not have enough brainpower to process the entirety of the information we encounter; therefore, we resort to shortcuts. Elite rhetoric can thus be influential because the public uses it as a shortcut in deciding what to think about a topic.

Although the public uses cues to understand the agenda set by elite rhetoric, this understanding is moderated by cognitive dissonance with the message (Kuklinski and Hurley 1994). As such, we can expect some people to have an adverse reaction to the rhetoric's intended message based on cues. I examine next the potential for identity to be a cue used by second-generation Americans in reacting negatively to Trump's intended message about the problems with illegal immigration. Throughout the book, I have called this process collateral damage, and in this chapter, I experimentally examine this effect using Trump's rhetoric.

Cues of Identity

The children of immigrants may see attacks on undocumented immigrants as an attack on a group with which they identify, and they will respond negatively to these attacks. Chapter 3 showed that Trump's rhetoric was consistently and thoroughly covered by the mass media for almost his entire time as a candidate and president, so almost every American will have some familiarity with his anti-immigration statements. Since Trump ran his campaign based on these ideas and subsequently won the nomination and the election, it may seem as though America supports these ideas because he won. Perceived discrimination is a dominant factor in increasing the salience of ethnic identity (Bernal et al. 1990). Therefore, it is highly possible that for the children of immigrants who hear a winning candidate vilifying immigrants, this rhetoric will act as a heuristic cue that the nation itself is also against them.

This possibility is related to the idea of linked fate, whereby one is connected to your group's fortunes—what happens to the individual is deeply intertwined with what happens to the group. Dawson (1994) described a black utility heuristic that creates group cohesion greater than what can be explained by raw materialist values, such as who benefits from tax policy. Because of the durability of this heuristic across multiple samples, researchers have recently investigated whether other people are similarly influenced by beliefs about a linked fate with their ethnic group (Masuoka and Sanchez 2010; Sanchez and Vargas 2016). The chief difference is that Hispanics and Asians are pan-ethnic groupings that combine many salient national ancestral origins, such as combining Korean Americans and Chinese Americans as Asian Americans or Cuban Americans and Mexican Americans as Latinos. Specifically relevant for this research, I show in chapter 7 that Vietnamese and Cuban Americans are different politically than other groups, which may be obscured when using pan-ethnic groupings. Nevertheless, there is still evidence of linked fate to the larger pan-ethnic grouping (Masuoka and Sanchez 2010).

Based on the prior literature on elite rhetoric and the powerful attachment of identity, I predict that exposure to Trump's anti-immigration rhetoric will decrease expressed patriotism and the importance of American identity for second-generation Americans. One way to test the predicted effect of Trump's rhetoric is to measure American identity and patriotism after exposure to it. Next, I examine how the likelihood for incorporation can be measured, suggesting that American identity and patriotism are reasonable proxies for the often difficult-to-measure concept.

Role of American Identity and Patriotism in Incorporation

This section shows how American identity[3] and patriotism are crucial for understanding the likelihood for incorporation and can be used as reliable proxy measures for it. The dependent variables I study below concern belonging to America. The literature in sociology shows how a sense of belonging is crucial for understanding why someone wants to incorporate—embracing an American identity and having feelings of patriotism toward America are measures of this feeling of belonging essential to gauging the likelihood that someone is willing to incorporate.

For example, in sociology, Lamont (2018) suggests that stigmatization resulting from hostile political rhetoric creates a barrier for stigmatized groups to see themselves as being welcomed into the greater community, which will impede incorporation. Becker (1963) shows that how we are labeled by society often influences our behavior. This sociological "labeling theory" suggests that having anti-immigration rhetoric label immigrants as distinct would, unlike other Americans, lower their likelihood of incorporating. These ideas are highly related to social identity theory (Tajfel 1978), which suggests that once social identities are created, human beings have a natural tendency to promote their in-group support and dislike the out-group. Anti-immigrant rhetoric that promotes immigrants to think of themselves as an unwelcome outsider group will simultaneously make immigrants and their children less likely to want to incorporate. At their core, these findings in sociology show that a sense of belonging is crucial to motivating joining groups. By measuring whether elite anti-immigration rhetoric lowers American identity and patriotism, we can use that to measure the likelihood that this person will subsequently want to incorporate with the greater society.

Even though American identity and patriotism are often considered

---

3. See Schildkraut (2014) for a detailed discussion of American identity, including its relationship to patriotism.

cultural attitudes, the negative impact from politicians' rhetoric is better described as an effect of incorporation processes rather than a lack of assimilation because it derives from elite action. It is essential to define the terms clearly to understand the causal mechanisms that derive from political rhetoric. Ramakrishnan (2013) states that incorporation is about inclusion (or exclusion) into organized groups' political processes, whereas assimilation is about immigrants' cultural change. While both definitions concern a fundamental belonging in American society, the chief distinction is how organized groups work to include or exclude immigrants into the broader society. Because the critical, independent variable is political rhetoric from elites in the Republican Party, I use the word incorporation throughout the book because this research is about how an organized group repulses the children of immigrants. The Republican Party and its leader Donald Trump have worked to convey strong messages that repulse second-generation Americans.

As we have seen, American identity and patriotism are crucial measures of involvement and engagement with American society. This is another way to say that American identity and patriotism are valid metrics for the broader concept of willingness to incorporate. American identity and patriotism serve as functional proxies for the grander concept of desire for incorporation into the larger society. Next, I examine the current levels of incorporation in the US.

Current Levels of Incorporation

Although cultural angst may exist over immigrant incorporation, the data show that incorporation is occurring among current second-generation Americans (Park and Myers 2010). Researchers find levels of incorporation based on objectively observed characteristics thought to be highly correlated with incorporation (Citrin et al. 2007; Kasinitz, Mollenkopf, and Waters 2005). Sociologists argue that even though it may seem trivial at first, the high adoption of American cultural traditions by immigrants and their children—such as playing baseball or baking turkeys for Thanksgiving—provides essential evidence of cultural incorporation (Alba and Nee 2003).

We also know from survey data that a level of expressed incorporation exists. For example, 60% of second-generation Americans view themselves as "typical Americans" and do not feel connected to their parents' home country (Pew Research Center 2014). A recent review of the evidence by a team of experts assembled by the National Academies of Sciences (2015) found that "across all measurable outcomes, integration increases over time, with immigrants becoming more like the native-born with more time in the country, and with the second and third generations becoming more like other native-born Americans than their parents were" (National Academies of Sciences 2015, 2).

Although this evidence based on traditional measures clearly shows that incorporation is occurring, a deep-rooted fear exists within American society that new immigrants will not truly become part of their new society (Huntington 2004). Several reasons have been suggested to explain why new immigrants might remain separate, such as easy access to international news and communication with family abroad and the general ability to remain abreast of events in their home country (see, e.g., Huntington 2004). Additionally, there is a fear that multiculturalism has created an intellectual justification and a supportive environment for nonincorporation (see, e.g., Schlesinger 1998).

Specifically, the fear is that while immigrants may speak English and succeed in educational environments, they are not genuinely patriotic and do not embrace an American identity, and consequently, they will not sacrifice for their country (see discussion in Segura 2006). Immigrants are often thought to be here simply for economic advantage or to escape troubles in their home country, and they are perceived as being unprepared to make profound sacrifices for the United States. At their core, justifications for mass-based patriotism center on shared sacrifice and overcoming problems through collective action. The concern is that a large percentage of the immigrant population is unwilling to sacrifice for the greater good, which would lead to free-riding on societal issues that require mutual sacrifice.

Evidence does not support such fears and concerns (see National Academies of Sciences 2015). Expressed patriotism from the children of immigrants is often as high or higher than from other Americans. For example, the 2012 American National Election Studies (ANES)[4]—which oversampled 1,000 Hispanic Americans—shows that rates of expressed patriotism and the importance placed on American identity are similar between those with two native-born parents and those with one or two foreign-born parents.[5]

However, certain factors can potentially alter the positive feelings

---

4. All models and figures in this book use the weights that come with the ANES.
5. These data are freely available at https://electionstudies.org/data-center/2012-time-series-study/

toward the United States that support the successful integration of the descendants of recent immigrants. Freedom of speech permits harsh rhetoric, and, as such, some politicians commonly engage in immigrant-bashing. Recently, however, there has been a surge in this rhetoric from politicians and political candidates in Europe and the United States. The collateral damage of this rhetoric on integration needs further study.

Predictions

Based on my theory described in chapter 2, I posit that second-generation Americans will express lower feelings of patriotism and the importance of American identity after exposure to anti-immigration rhetoric. Trump's rhetoric has focused on three main problems with undocumented immigrants: (1) committing crimes, (2) taking jobs, and (3) not assimilating or not being patriotic. The crucial point is that by focusing public attention on problems 1 and 2, Trump may himself bolster problem 3. Trump's rhetoric may exacerbate the very problem he laments by making America seem hostile to immigrants and their children, thus provoking an adverse reaction from people connected to the immigrant community.

Experimental Procedures

To test these predictions, an online sample of second-generation Americans was recruited to take a survey online for a $5 cash incentive through Qualtrics in April 2016.[6] The sample was drawn from a pool of over 5 million potential respondents and then matched to 2010 census data for second-generation Americans regarding age, gender, income, and education. Participants also had to be 18 and a US citizen with two foreign-born parents. The usual caveats about the lack of representativeness of the sample due to the nature of who is online and willing to fill out a survey for a cash payment apply. Nevertheless, these samples have been shown to have a great deal of similarity to more traditional nationally representative samples (see Mullinix et al. 2015). Online samples that have been matched to Census characteristics have shown predictability to political outcomes where there are objective data that they can be compared against. Based

---

6. One factor to note is that this experiment was conducted before the Trump presidency—while many of the arguments and data compare the different presidents and their anti-immigrant rhetoric. In chapter 6, I analyze experiments conducted during his presidency and find similar results.

on their common usage in modern social science and proven validity, these online samples will sufficiently represent the second-generation American population. Participants filled out the survey online after being randomly assigned to read a description of Trump's rhetoric about illegal immigration, his rhetoric about free trade, or a text about bird watching (the control group).

The reason for including the treatment with Trump's rhetoric on free trade pertained to possible bundling. Confounding occurs when a treatment contains more than one element that may work as stimuli on the dependent variable. Trump was a well-known celebrity who had made many statements that had nothing to do with immigration but still may make someone who does not like those statements less patriotic or less caring about having an American identity. Similarly, he was the nominee of the Republican Party, which has a recent history of being anti-immigrant, separate from the influence of Trump's rhetoric. If I only provided one treatment, it would bundle Trump's rhetoric with these other salient factors. To control this confounding, I provide another stimulus that contains all of these features—Trump, the Republican Party, and so forth—but does not mention immigration. I can then compare the influence on the dependent variable with and without anti-immigration rhetoric. I included one manipulation check to ensure that the participants read the treatment, but the results are similar if all participants are included.

Data

The data come from a questionnaire that all participants completed. See the survey questionnaire in appendix table A2 and a table of summary statistics by treatment conditions in appendix table A1. Table A1 also compares means t-test with no significant differences for being Asian American, Hispanic, or male or according to income, age, education, or political ideology.

Stimuli

The stimuli were designed to accurately describe Trump's policy opinions as stated on his campaign website. The first treatment describes his aim to build a wall on the border with Mexico and his view that illegal immigrants commit crimes and take jobs away from Americans. Here is the first treatment:

> **Trump-Immigration:** Donald Trump is the leading candidate for the Republican Party's nomination for president. He opposes illegal immigration and wants to build a wall to keep out those coming in illegally from Mexico. He says that illegal immigrants commit crimes and take jobs away from Americans.

I also provided another treatment about Trump that was not about immigration policy but international trade, which was also central to his campaign. Policies were also mentioned on his website about scrapping international trade deals and fighting currency manipulation. Here is the alternative treatment:

> **Trump-Trade:** Donald Trump is the leading candidate for the Republican Party's nomination for president. He is opposed to current international free trade deals and wants to scrap these deals or renegotiate them. He says that the countries in these deals commit currency manipulation against the United States dollar and take jobs away from Americans.

These stimuli are accurate statements of the candidate's position that were often stated and commonly reported in the mass media. There was also a control group that read a similarly sized story about an unrelated nonpolitical topic.[7]

Dependent Variables

The dependent variables were designed to measure the two most salient and controversial aspects of immigrant integration: patriotism and attachment to American identity. Wording for both questions was taken directly from the ANES.

> **Patriotism:** How do you feel about the United States of America? Hate it (coded 0), Dislike it (1), Neither like nor dislike it (2), Like it (3), Love it (4).
> **American Identity:** How important is being an American to you personally? Extremely important (coded 5), Very important (4),

---

7. The topic for the control group was birdwatching, and you can read the text in the appendix.

Somewhat important (3), A little important (2), Not at all important (1).

Manipulation Check

A manipulation check was shown immediately after the participant read the stimulus, and the software did not allow them to reread. It asked one of these questions after each corresponding condition: "According to the passage that you just read, birdwatching has recently become? Less popular, Very popular, I did not read it carefully"; "According to the passage that you just read, Donald Trump says countries in these free trade deals do what to the United States? Manipulate currency, abuse human rights, I did not read it carefully"; and "According to the passage that you just read, Donald Trump says illegal immigrants do what? Commit crimes, Get welfare, I did not read it carefully." Seventeen out of 183 in the control condition could not answer the question correctly, while 39 out of 179 in the trade condition and 27 out of 179 in the immigration condition could not answer the question correctly. I checked the results by including those who could not answer this manipulation check correctly, and the coefficients were similar and in the same direction. For simplicity, I include the models with those who could answer the manipulation check.

Results

The impact of Trump's rhetoric on second-generation Americans' attitudes was small but significant for both dependent variables. For simplicity, I show the treatment effect graphically below. Note that, overall, the expressed patriotism and American identity were very high for all groups in this sample. These levels are similar to the 2012 ANES data for respondents who stated they have two foreign-born parents, suggesting some generalizability for this online sample.

Figure 12 shows a statistically significant decrease in expressed patriotism for the group exposed to Trump's anti-immigration rhetoric. There was no corresponding decrease in expressed patriotism for the group exposed to Trump's rhetoric on trade. The size of the effect, however, was not very large. The Trump immigrant condition averaged 0.2 lower than the control group in expressed patriotism on a 0–4 scale. This decrease is about a quarter of a standard deviation. However, it is possible that a linear effect could exist whereby repeated exposure to this type of rhetoric would further decrease expressed patriotism.

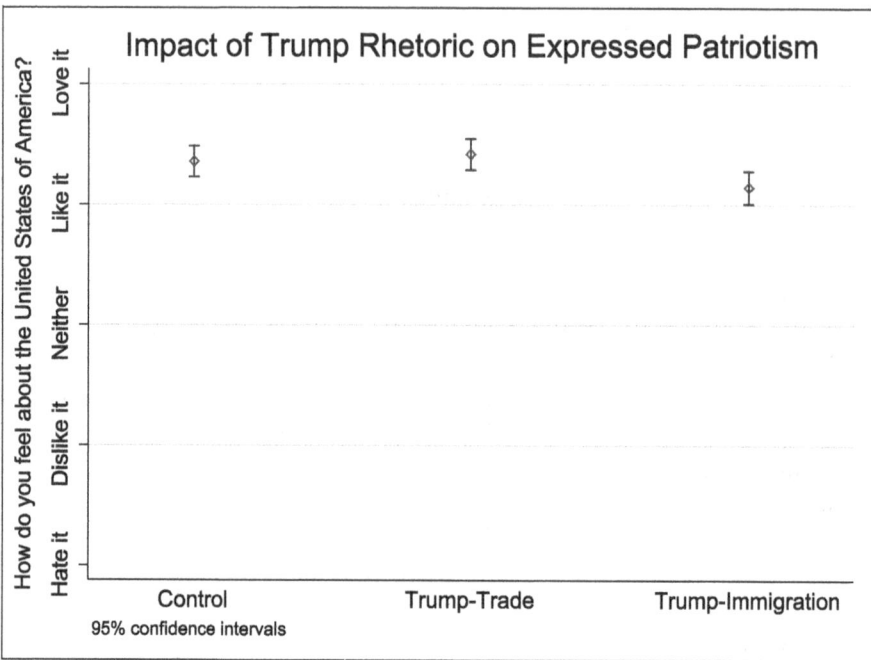

Fig. 12. Results of exposure to the experimental stimuli for all three conditions for patriotism.

To better understand this effect, it helps to examine a histogram distribution of the dependent variable by treatment conditions. Figure 13 shows the histogram of the dependent variable divided by each treatment condition. The most significant effect was a decrease in the number of respondents in the Trump immigrant condition who expressed extreme love of America, which was the highest value for the patriotism variable. A 10-percentage point decrease was found among those who expressed extreme love compared with the control group.

The results for expressed importance of American identity were similar. Figure 14 shows that the treatment group exposed to Trump's anti-immigration rhetoric had a statistically significant decrease in American identity's expressed importance. Again, the effect was not large, and the substantive effect of this brief exposure only lowered the importance of American identity a small amount. The Trump immigration condition averaged 0.23 lower than the control group in expressed American identity on a 1–5 scale. This decrease is also about a quarter of a standard deviation.

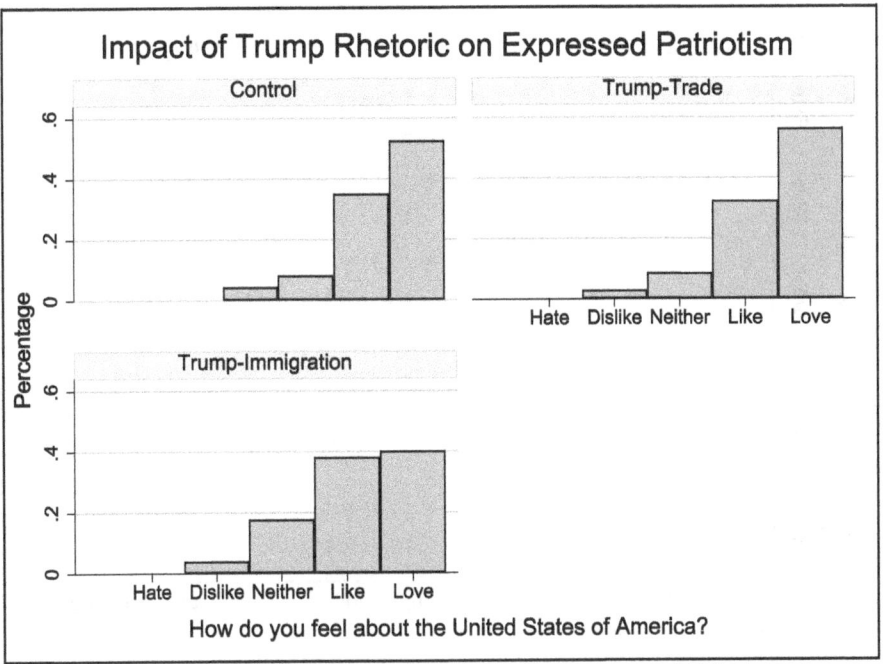

Fig. 13. Histogram of exposure to the experimental stimuli for all three conditions for patriotism.

Figure 15 shows the histogram of American Identity by treatment condition, and again the highest category showed the greatest effect. There was an approximately 10 percentage point drop among those who expressed extreme importance of having an American identity. Thus, the negative effect of exposure to Trump's anti-immigration rhetoric was similar for both patriotism and American identity.

Table 5 shows ordered logistic regression models of the dependent variables regressed on the treatment conditions. Both models in Table 5 show that the effect is statistically significant under that specification as well.

Results by Ethnicity of Participant

Trump specifically mentioned Hispanic Americans often, and they are directly mentioned by Huntington (2004) as not assimilating. Since the assimilation of Hispanic Americans generates great turmoil in American politics, it is interesting to take a closer look at the results for this subpopu-

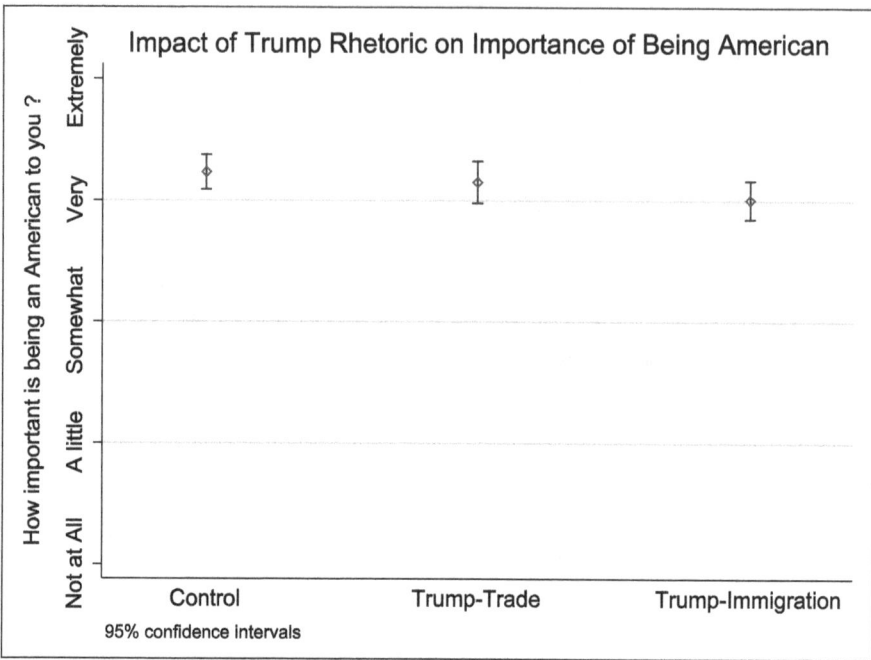

Fig. 14. Results of treatment effects for all three conditions for American identity.

lation. Table 6 shows the effects between random assignment to the three treatment conditions interacted with being Hispanic. No significant effects for being Hispanic and assignment to treatment were apparent for any of the dependent variables. This outcome suggests that this subpopulation's reaction to Trump's rhetoric matches other types of immigrants in this sample.

Asian Americans are another large immigrant group that is sometimes perceived as preferring to remain distinct and accused of not assimilating. Table 7 shows the effects between the treatment conditions and being Asian American. Here, the results show no significant effect for being Asian American and assignment to treatment for either dependent variable.

These outcomes suggest that the impact of elite anti-immigration rhetoric on matters of American identity and patriotism matched that for other types of immigrants in this sample. Another plausible interpretation is that since only 32% of the sample was Hispanic (160 participants) and Asian Americans were 20% (100), data may have been insufficient to investigate these subpopulations divided into three conditions. Again, unfortunately,

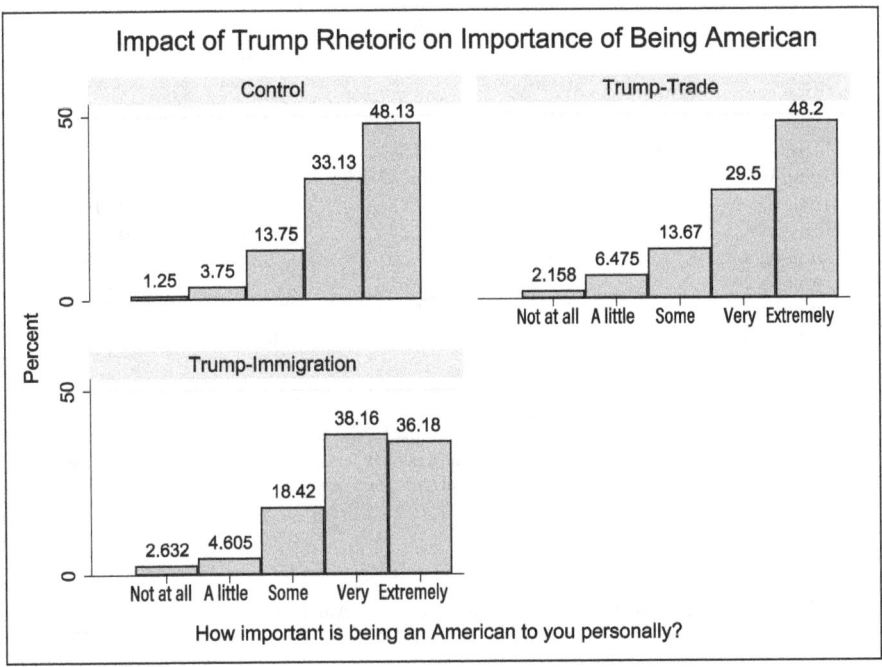

Fig. 15. Histogram of treatment effects for all three conditions for American identity.

TABLE 5. Ordered Logistic Regression Models of Treatment Effect

Variable	Patriotism	(S.E.)	American Identity	(S.E.)
Trump-Immigration	−0.526*	0.215	−0.447*	0.209
Trump-Trade	0.141	0.224	−0.082	0.219
Cut point 1	−3.416***	0.280	−4.089***	0.360
Cut point 2	−1.875***	0.183	−2.800***	0.225
Cut point 3	−0.109	0.154	−1.446***	0.167
Cut point 4			0.060	0.151
N	451		451	
χ^2	10.219**		5.128	

Note: This table shows the results of ordered logistic regression models for treatment condition for each dependent variable for participants who could correctly answer the manipulation check question.
*$p < .05$, **$p < .01$, ***$p < .001$

TABLE 6. Ordered Probit Regression Models for Hispanic Americans

Variable	Patriotism	S.E.	American Identity	S.E.
Hispanic × Trump Imm.	0.528	0.360	−0.010	0.360
Hispanic × Trump Trade	0.857*	0.387	0.066	0.375
Trump Immigration	−0.533*	0.215	−0.411*	0.208
Trump Trade	−0.282	0.221	−0.383	0.214
Hispanic	−0.433	0.253	0.147	0.256
Cut point 1	−2.056***	0.207	−2.293***	0.238
Cut point 2	−1.311***	0.175	−1.742***	0.189
Cut point 3	−0.097	0.159	−0.913***	0.160
Cut point 4			0.069	0.153
N	243		243	
χ^2	10.256		8.305	

Note: This table shows the results for assignment treatment condition for each dependent variable for participants who could correctly answer the manipulation check question.
*$p < .05$, **$p < .01$, ***$p < .001$

TABLE 7. Ordered Probit Regression Models for Asian Americans

Variable	Patriotism	S.E.	American Identity	S.E.
Asian × Trump Imm.	−0.388	0.435	0.136	0.427
Asian × Trump Trade	−0.010	0.461	0.165	0.444
Trump Immigration	−0.262	0.191	−0.448*	0.190
Trump Trade	0.009	0.199	−0.404*	0.196
Asian	−0.067	0.310	−0.389	0.302
Cut point 1	−1.891***	0.187	−2.411***	0.227
Cut point 2	−1.157***	0.154	−1.870***	0.177
Cut point 3	0.052	0.140	−1.047***	0.149
Cut point 4			−0.057	0.139
N	243		243	
χ^2	7.398		9.863	

Note: This table shows the results for assignment treatment condition for each dependent variable for participants who could correctly answer the manipulation check question.
*$p < .05$, **$p < .01$, ***$p < .001$

due to data limitations, I cannot test subethnic groupings, such as the difference between Cuban Americans and Mexican Americans or Vietnamese Americans and Korean Americans in exposure to the treatment effect. In chapter 7, I also examine the differences between these national ethnic groupings.

Checking Results for External Validity with ANES Survey Data

The causal inference derived from these experiments provides an exact test of Trump's rhetoric. It is also interesting to study the impact of this rhetoric on second-generation Americans outside of controlled experimental conditions. One way to do this is to examine nationally representative survey data from 2012 and 2016 to determine if similar correlations exist between being a second-generation American and their feelings toward America when Trump was on the ballot or not.

To augment these experimental results with additional evidence, I pool 2012 and 2016 ANES survey data to show that the experimental evidence's basic correlations are replicated in nationally representative survey data. The ANES survey data do not directly measure exposure to Trump's rhetoric, but the experiments in this chapter show that this rhetoric does have a direct effect. The correlations below test whether second-generation Americans have negative feelings of American identity and when seeing the American flag flying. This latter measure was how the ANES measured patriotism in 2012 and 2016. While it is not an optimal measure, it is the only measure of patriotism available in these data. Here is the wording of the specific questions used in table 8:

American Identity—
How important is being American to your identity?
1. Extremely important; 2. Very important; 3. Moderately important; 4. A little important; 5. Not at all important

Patriotism—When you see the American flag flying, does it make you feel good, bad, or neither good nor bad?
1. Extremely good; 2. Moderately good; 3. A little good; 4. A little bad; 5. Moderately bad; 6. Extremely bad

TABLE 8. Determinants of Patriotism and American Identity in 2012 and 2016

Variable	Patriotism	S.E.	American Identity	S.E.
Trump on ballot	−0.734**	0.250	−1.073***	0.249
Age	0.034***	0.005	0.025***	0.005
Education	−0.178**	0.054	−0.061	0.053
Income	0.005	0.008	0.001	0.008
Black	−0.538**	0.201	0.101	0.201
Hispanic	0.052	0.149	0.371*	0.150
Female	0.023	0.115	0.085	0.115
Cut point 1	−3.682***	0.291	−3.356***	0.284
Cut point 2	−2.630***	0.251	−2.325***	0.246
Cut point 3	−1.100***	0.232	−1.069***	0.231
Cut point 4	0.231	0.229	0.381	0.229
N	1,066		1,066	
χ^2	85.531***		37.622***	

Note: Cells represent unstandardized coefficients and standard errors for ordered logistic regression models for determinants of patriotism and American identity. Patriotism is measured with question on feelings when seeing the American flag coded from (1) very bad to (5) very good. The American identity variable is a standard five-part Likert scale, coded from feeling no importance being American (1) to feeling extremely important to be American coded (5).

+$p < .10$, *$p < .05$, **$p < .01$, ***$p < .001$

The results in table 8 clearly show that being a second-generation American correlates with lower rates of patriotism and the importance of American identity when Trump was on the ballot in 2016. This shows that the experiment's results, obtained in additional survey data, that having a communication environment defined by Trump's anti-immigration rhetoric was deleterious on second-generation Americans' feelings of American identity and emotions when seeing the American flag flying. The primary findings gain greater external validity by replicating the experimental results with nationally representative survey data from years with and without Trump as a nominee.

Conclusion

This chapter finds that even brief exposure to anti-immigrant elite rhetoric lowers second-generation Americans' expressed patriotism and American identity. The results are from a survey experiment conducted with an online sample of US-born adult children of immigrants matched to nationally representative census data for this group and backed up with 2016

ANES survey data. After second-generation Americans are exposed to a description of Trump's anti-immigration rhetoric, there is a statistically significant drop in expressed patriotism and feelings about the importance of having an American identity. By including a second treatment group, I also showed that the drop was not due to Trump himself, the Republican Party, or any other related stimuli; it was the actual rhetoric that caused the effect. The effect was not greater for Hispanic or Asian Americans, and I will explore this in greater detail in chapter 7. One limitation of this experimental research is that it does not allow interpretation of the effects over time. It could be that these effects dissipate quickly or even rise in importance over time. The current data does not allow us to test these possibilities.

The baseline for second-generation Americans is high levels of expressed patriotism and the importance of their American identity. However, the rhetoric did have a substantively small but significant effect in lowering these feelings. The treatment was designed not to be excessively belligerent toward immigrants. Trump sends many tweets a day, often about immigrants, combined with other exposure from all traditional and social media that contain Trump's anti-immigration rhetoric. Thus, we may expect that the relatively small substantive effect that I found manifests even more in the actual population. In other words, while one brief treatment leads to a small effect, the election and Trump's presidency potentially exposed second-generation Americans to thousands of similar stimuli of at least equal length and strength. Although we cannot define any threshold effects for prolonged exposure, these treatments may be thought of as similar to the arguments brought by scholars of the minimal group paradigm. As Tajfel (1970) famously argued, if there are effects in a minimal experimental setting, then in a real-world setting, where the treatment is more powerful, we can be relatively sure to find an effect.

The majority of these second-generation Americans love America and are very patriotic. A long series of prior inputs influence patriotism, and any president's rhetoric will mix and blend in with personal experiences, parents' attitudes, and other political socialization factors. These American citizens mostly grew up in the United States and received many prior inputs before Trump was president that emphasized patriotism, such as saying the Pledge of Allegiance in public schools; they start at a high baseline of patriotism. However, the crucial point is that exposure to Trump's rhetoric lowered patriotism from this high level. The experimental stimuli are designed to be relatively noncontroversial compared to some of the more extreme comments that Trump has made (see chapter 4 for examples). More importantly, Trump made hundreds of tweets, which are recycled through thousands of media stories. The experiment only measures the treatment effect of a small bit of rhetoric. The fact that it shows a negative impact is suggestive that the grand total effect of Trump long term will be negative. These second-generation Americans will end up being patriotic after the Trump presidency as the results do not suggest that the impact of Trump's presidency will make them dislike or even hate America. However, the impact of lowering patriotism from his rhetoric is clear from these results, and while they may still have a relatively high level of American identity and patriotism, they will probably be lower after his presidency. Another critical issue is that the experiment does not have enough data to disaggregate the results by groups such as Venezuelans or Colombians, so we cannot make any statements as to how the results would differentiate by these groups.

The following chapter is an extension of these results and their implications for American political parties.

References

Alba, Richard, and Victor Nee. 2003. *Remaking the American Mainstream: Incorporation and Contemporary Immigration*. Cambridge, MA: Harvard University Press.

Becker, Howard S. 1963. *Outsiders: Studies in the Sociology of Deviance*. New York: Macmillan.

Bennett, W. Lance. 1990. "Toward a Theory of Press-State Relations in the United States." *Journal of Communication* 40 (2): 103–27.

Bennett, W. Lance, Regina Lawrence, and Steven Livingston. 2006. "None Dare Call It Torture: Indexing and the Limits of Press Independence in the Abu Ghraib Scandal." *Journal of Communication* 56 (3): 467–85.

Bernal, Martha E., George P. Knight, Camille A. Garza, Katheryn A. Ocampo, and Marya K. Costa. 1990. "The Development of Ethnic Identity in Mexican-American Children." *Hispanic Journal of Behavioral Sciences* 12 (1): 3–24.

Campbell, Karlyn Kohrs, and Kathleen Hall Jamieson. 2008. *Presidents Creating the Presidency: Deed Done in Words*. Chicago: University of Chicago Press.

Citrin, Jack, Amy Lerman, Michael Murakami, and Kathryn Pearson. 2007. "Testing Huntington: Is Hispanic Immigration a Threat to American Identity?" *Perspectives on Politics* 5 (1): 31–48.

Dawson, Michael. 1994. *Behind the Mule: Race and Class in African American Politics*. Princeton: Princeton University Press.

Edwards, George C., III. 1996. "Presidential Rhetoric: What Difference Does It Make?" In *Beyond the Rhetorical Presidency*, edited by Martin J. Medhurst, College Station: Texas A&M University Press.

Edwards, George C., III. 2003. *On Deaf Ears: The Limits of the Bully Pulpit.* New Haven: Yale University Press.

Huddy, Leonie, and Nadia Khatib. 2007. "American Patriotism, National Identity, and Political Involvement." *American Journal of Political Science* 51 (1): 63–77.

Huntington, Samuel P. 2004. "The Hispanic Challenge." *Foreign Policy* (March–April): 30–45.

Kasinitz, Philip, John H. Mollenkopf, and Mary C. Waters, eds. 2005. *Becoming New Yorkers: Ethnographies of the New Second Generation.* New York: Russell Sage.

Kernell, Samuel. 1997. *Going Public.* 3rd ed. Washington, DC: CQ Press.

Kuklinski, James H., and Norman L. Hurley. 1994. "On Hearing and Interpreting Political Messages: A Cautionary Tale of Citizen Cue-Taking." *Journal of Politics* 56 (3): 729–51.

Lamont, Michèle. 2018. "Addressing Recognition Gaps: Destigmatization and the Reduction of Inequality." *American Sociological Review* 83 (3): 419–44.

Lupia, Arthur. 1994. "Shortcuts versus Encyclopedias: Information and Voting Behavior in California Insurance Reform Elections." *American Political Science Review* 88 (1): 63–76.

Lupia, Arthur, and Mathew D. McCubbins. 1998. *The Democratic Dilemma: Can Citizens Learn What They Need to Know?* Cambridge: Cambridge University Press.

Masuoka, Natalie, and Gabriel Sanchez. 2010. "Brown-Utility Heuristic? The Presence and Contributing Factors of Latino Linked Fate." *Hispanic Journal of Behavioral Sciences* 32 (4): 519–31.

Mollenkopf, John, and Jennifer Hochschild. 2010. "Immigrant Political Incorporation: Comparing Success in the United States and Western Europe." *Ethnic and Racial Studies* 33 (1): 19–38.

Mullinix, Kevin J., Thomas J. Leeper, James N. Druckman, and Jeremy Freese. 2015. "The Generalizability of Survey Experiments." *Journal of Experimental Political Science* 2:109–38.

National Academies of Sciences, Engineering, and Medicine. 2015. *The Integration of Immigrants into American Society.* Washington, DC: National Academies Press. https://doi.org/10.17226/21746

Ono, Kent A., and John M. Sloop. 2004. *Shifting Borders: Rhetoric, Immigration, and California's Proposition 187.* Philadelphia: Temple University Press.

Park, Julie, and Dowell Myers. 2010. "Intergenerational Mobility in the Post-1965 Immigration Era: Estimates by an Immigrant Generation Cohort Method." *Demography* 47 (May): 369–92.

Pew Research Center. 2014. *Second-Generation Americans: A Portrait of the Adult Children of Immigrants.* https://www.pewsocialtrends.org/wp-content/uploads/sites/3/2013/02/FINAL_immigrant_generations_report_2-7-13.pdf

Popkin, Samuel L. 1991. *The Reasoning Voter: Communication and Persuasion in Presidential Campaigns.* Chicago: University of Chicago Press.

Portes, Alejandro, and Rubén G. Rumbaut. 2001. *Legacies: The Story of the Immigrant Second Generation.* Berkeley: University of California Press.

Ramakrishnan, S. Karthick. 2004. "Second-Generation Immigrants? The '2.5 Generation' in the United States." *Social Science Quarterly* 85 (2): 380–99.

Ramakrishnan, S. Karthick. 2013. "Incorporation versus Assimilation: The Need for Conceptual Differentiation." In *Outsiders No More: Models of Immigrant Political Incorporation*, by Jennifer Hochschild, Jacqueline Chattopadhyay, Claudine Gay, and Michael Jones-Correa. New York: Oxford University Press.

Sanchez, Gabriel R., and Edward D. Vargas. 2016. "Taking a Closer Look at Group Identity: The Link between Theory and Measurement of Group Consciousness and Linked Fate." *Political Research Quarterly* 69 (1): 160–74.

Schildkraut, Deborah J. 2014. "Boundaries of American Identity: Evolving Understandings of 'Us'." *Annual Review of Political Science* 17 (1): 441–60.

Schlesinger, Arthur Meier. 1998. *The Disuniting of America: Reflections on a Multicultural Society*. New York: W. W. Norton.

Schneider, Saundra K., and William G. Jacoby. 2005. "Elite Discourse and American Public Opinion: The Case of Welfare Spending." *Political Research Quarterly* 58 (3): 367–79.

Segura, Gary M. 2006. "Symposium Introduction: Immigration and National Identity." *Perspectives on Politics* 4 (1): 277–78.

Tajfel, Henri. 1970. "Experiments in Intergroup Discrimination." *Scientific American* 223:96–102.

Tajfel, Henri. 1978. "The Achievement of Inter-group Differentiation." In *Differentiation between Social Groups*, edited by Henri Tajfel, 77–100. London: Academic Press.

Tulis, Jeffrey. 1988. *The Rhetorical Presidency*. Princeton: Princeton University Press.

CHAPTER 6

Rhetoric and Attitudes toward the Republican Party and Donald Trump

Overstating the importance of partisan identification would be difficult. Through decades of studies, political science researchers have consistently found that it matters in a way that almost no other factor in politics does (e.g., Campbell et al. 1960). The extremely high correlation between party identification and vote choice has remained exceptionally strong since the beginning of the survey era in the 1940s (Berelson, Lazarsfeld, and McPhee 1954). However, the influence of party identification goes far beyond vote choice. Party identification colors how we select information (Jerit and Barabas 2012) and view information (Taber and Lodge 2006). It also influences with whom we discuss politics (McPherson, Smith-Lovin, and Cook 2001) and whether we choose to be involved at all. Jennings and Niemi (1981) found that only about a third of Americans will ever change their party identification. Once we have an allegiance with a political party, it becomes a defining factor in how we interact with the political world throughout most of our lives.

Interestingly, a large and growing number of Americans are not attached to any party (Clarke and Stewart 1998). This lack of attachment is particularly apparent among second-generation Americans, and long-standing sociological theories explain the underlying reasons (Hajnal and Lee 2011). The literature on political socialization shows that the primary determinant of one's political party's is a transfer of beliefs from parent to child (Jennings and Niemi 1974). This transfer occurs in both explicit and implicit ways. Explicitly, parents often discuss politics, including in conversations with their children. In doing so, they convey ideological positions and general support for candidates, indicating a clear partisan direction. Children can infer which party they should support based on political discussions between parents and with parents.

Lee (2008a) argued that the following five factors link identity to politics: definition, identification, consciousness, venue selection, and choice. By attacking immigrants, Trump's rhetoric triggers increased consciousness of immigrant identity by focusing attention on immigration and politicizing it. Due to their feelings of linked fate, second-generation Americans may be alienated from a political party with anti-immigration policies and rhetoric. This chapter's primary argument is that anti-immigration rhetoric will strengthen group identity among second-generation Americans, leading them to counter and oppose the Republican Party.

Partisan Recruitment and Partisan Estrangement

Hero (1992) described the immigrant political condition as "two-tiered pluralism," in which immigrants have legal rights and formal inclusion but are marginalized by a lack of mobilization from both parties. Many in the Republican Party, such as Karl Rove, have argued that Republicans should recruit second-generation Americans (see Rove 2013). They highlighted that the party has an ideological agreement on many issues with second-generation Americans and that a base level of social conservativism exists within this group. These Republicans make the argument that second-generation Americans are a potential source of new party members.

Andersen (2008) explained that recruitment into a party only happens when it does not endanger current party factions. The Republican Party is in a bind because if it softens its rhetoric on immigration, it may lose members. After all, many Republicans voters are anti-immigrant. As Wong et al. (2011, 122) noted, "For the most part, scholars conclude that today's parties lack the organizational capacity, the cultural literacy, and perhaps even the political motivation to shepherd new immigrants into the political process and nurture secure attachments with a particular political party." So, even if some Republicans want to mobilize this group, many other Republicans lack the will and resources to do so and often do not (see Wong 2008). Instead, the modern Republican Party led by President Trump has focused on base-mobilization strategies that often use anti-immigration rhetoric. For example, former senator Jeff Sessions embodies the anti-immigration rhetoric of the modern Republican Party. Sessions said that "since 1965,"

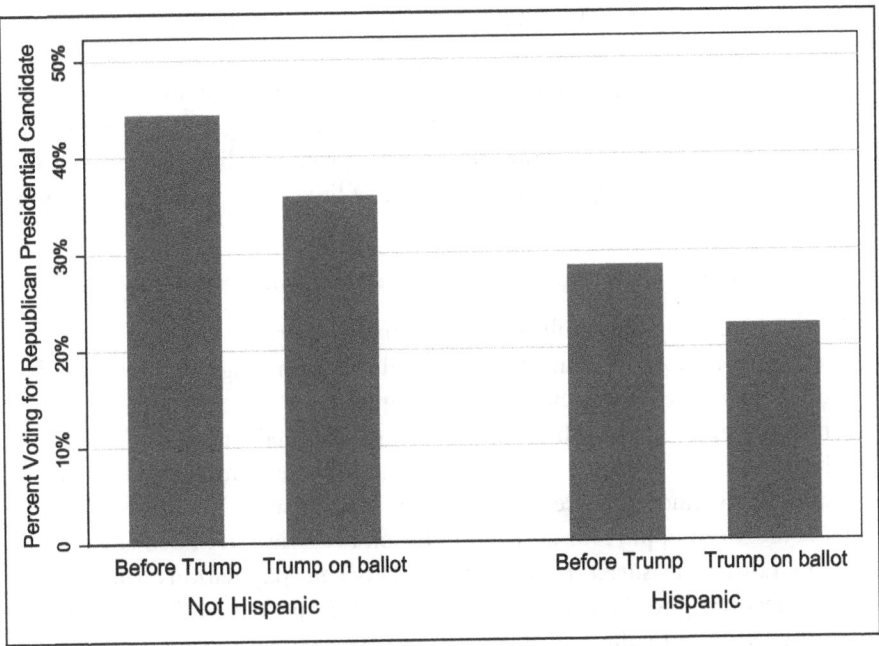

Fig. 16. Feelings of governmental trust of second-generation Americans, 1980 to 2016.

there has been an "extreme, unprecedented pattern of immigration . . . unlike most established countries in the world" (Sessions 2017). This rhetoric may lead to a partisan estrangement between the Republican Party and second-generation Americans rather than partisan recruitment.

Many second-generation Americans support incorporation generally and are likely to eventually join political parties if they are unencumbered by pressure to stay out. However, incorporation requires both the receiving political party to accept immigrants and the immigrants to desire incorporation. Massey and Sanchez (2010, 11) described this two-way process as "natives control interactions with outsiders by creating institutional, social, psychological, and spatial mechanisms that delimit immigrants' access to material resources and even social status. Immigrants construct identities based on how they perceive and respond to these social boundaries." Scholars often assume that parties work to get immigrants to identify with them, but other outcomes are possible. How recent immigrants react to current rhetoric may dramatically shape American politics in the next century.

To test the impact of anti-immigration rhetoric on second-generation

Americans' partisan attachment, I conducted two survey experiments where I randomly assigned anti-immigration rhetoric expressed by President Trump. This experiment presupposes that second-generation Americans care about immigration and the treatment of immigrants. In the next section, I show empirically that they have a profound disagreement with Trump's ideas on immigration and feelings of linked fate with immigrants.

Support for Trump's Ideas and Linked Fate with Immigrants

Before examining the results of a 2017 survey experiment on this topic, it is essential to note that the sample of children of immigrants was paired with a sample of children of nonimmigrants. In other words, people whose parents were both born outside the United States and people whose parents were both born in the United States completed the same survey. By including these two groups of participants, I could compare basic ideas on support for anti-immigration rhetoric and linked fate with immigrants—measured pretreatment—between populations that differed according to their parents' background. Importantly, this approach ensured that individuals with immigrant parents were not assumed to necessarily and automatically be pro-immigration and those born to nonimmigrant parents not to be inherently viewed as anti-immigration. Indeed, Trump was one of the least popular presidents in US history (Gallup 2021), so it is highly plausible that many people with parents born in the United States do not like his rhetoric. These data make it possible to compare and examine any disproportionate support from having both parents born outside the United States.

Figure 17 shows that second-generation Americans intensely disliked Trump's immigration ideas by about 20 percentage points more than those who are not second-generation Americans.[1] Trump's ideas were generally unpopular within both groups, but the dislike was much stronger among second-generation Americans. Indeed, only 5% of second-generation Americans strongly agreed with Trump's ideas compared to 16% of non-second-generation Americans. This result indicates that Trump's rhetoric may repulse second-generation Americans more than Americans who do not have immigrant parents. Anti-immigration rhetoric was extremely unpopular within this group, providing evidence for a direct causal mecha-

---

1. The question was worded as "What do you think of Donald Trump's ideas on immigration? I fully agree with his ideas, I somewhat agree with his ideas, I somewhat disagree with his ideas, and I fully disagree with his ideas."

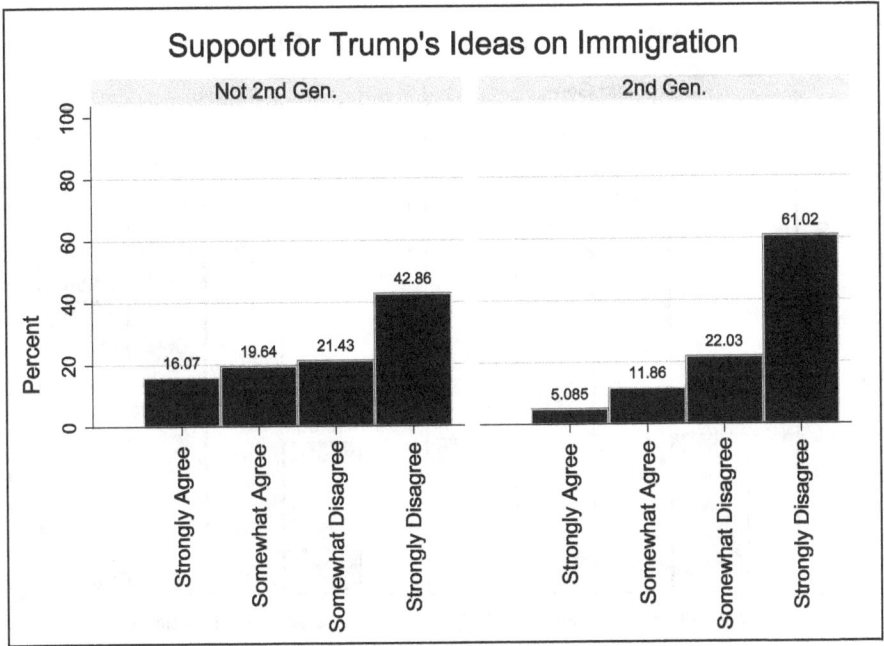

Fig. 17. Levels of agreement with Trump's ideas on immigration by second-generation and non-second-generation Americans.

nism by which this group will have a lower partisan identification with the Republican Party.

Another relevant topic is the concept of linked fate. Linked fate is a feeling of attachment to a larger group such that one's fate is linked with the fate of the larger group. Figure 18 shows that individuals with both parents born outside the United States had greater feelings of a linked fate with immigrants than those with both parents born in the United States.[2] Twenty-four percent of second-generation Americans felt their fate is closely linked with immigrants' fate, whereas 18% of non-second-generation Americans also felt this way. The level in the latter group was high, and it shows the potential limits of anti-immigration rhetoric. The result may also be at least partly influenced by social desirability bias. It is well known that survey respondents often give responses that they think

2. The question was worded as "How much of what happens to immigrants in this country will have something to do with what happens in your life? What happens to immigrants will affect you a lot, some, not very much, or not at all?"

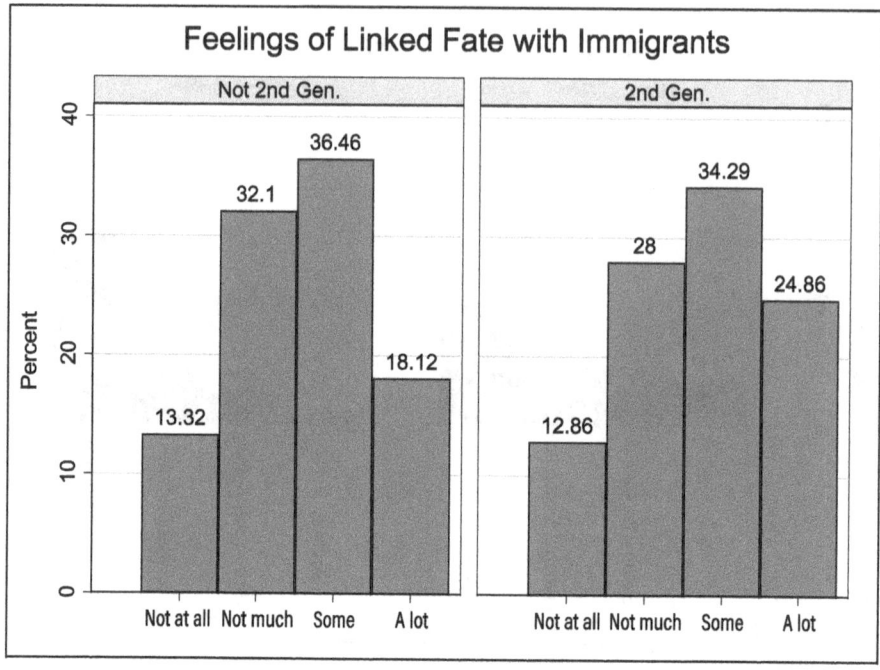

Fig. 18. Agreement with the respondent having a linked fate with immigrants by second-generation and non-second-generation Americans.

are socially desirable. Consequently, it is plausible that since respect for others and acceptance of diversity are strongly promoted within the education system, respondents understood that it is socially desirable to claim a linked fate with immigrants.

Despite this relatively high rate of linked fate expressed by non-second-generation Americans, a disproportionate level of linked fate was found with second-generation Americans. A full 60% of second-generation Americans believed that their fate is linked some or a lot with immigrants.' Since they are US citizens, they would have also gone through the same educational processes and socialization that non-second-generation Americans experienced. Although the level of linked fate was not much higher, a full majority of second-generation Americans believed they had a linked fate with immigrants. We can expect that if Trump is attacking immigrants, these Americans would feel as though he is attacking them.

Due to its anti-immigration rhetoric, the Republican Party stands to lose a good portion of the fastest-growing demographic group in America, second-generation Americans. In America's current evenly matched and basically tied electoral environment, the loss of even 1 or 2 percentage points of the electorate would potentially change several presidential elections. This loss will hold if negative political communication impedes political incorporation and alters political allegiances (see Kim 2007). Lee (2008b) shows that the linked fate attitudinal process shown for African Americans exists among immigrants and possibly extends to their children. If so, we may expect that people who feel linked to a group's fate will be alienated by rhetoric antagonistic toward that group. Therefore, if anti-immigration rhetoric is associated with a political party, second-generation Americans may turn against that party.

Next, I detail my predictions, experimental procedures, and data. Afterward, I analyze the results.

Predictions

Based on my theory, I predict that exposure to Trump's anti-immigration rhetoric would cause second-generation Americans to be less likely to support the Republican Party. Further, I predict that even if second-generation immigrants identified as conservative, this exposure would cause them to be less likely to have a Republican Party identification.[3] I also expect that exposure to Trump's anti-immigration rhetoric would lower their approval for Trump's performance as president. Additionally, I predict that the impact of Trump's rhetoric would not differ between second-generation Hispanic and Asian Americans because these groups have similar levels of linked fate with immigrants. Consequently, they are likely to be affected by anti-immigration rhetoric in the same general direction. In summary, the five expectations of this chapter are the following:

- Exposure to Trump's anti-immigration rhetoric will lead to less support for the Republican Party among second-generation Americans.
- Exposure to Trump's anti-immigration rhetoric will lead to less support for the Republican Party among conservative second-generation Americans.
- Exposure to Trump's anti-immigration rhetoric will lead to a similar reduction in support for the Republican Party between second-generation Hispanic and Asian Americans.
- Exposure to Trump's anti-immigration rhetoric will lower approv-

---

3. To be clear, this predicted loss of support will be present on average across all elections, not necessarily present for any specific candidate or electoral cycle, which of course, may have split-ticket voting or even temporary party-switching.

al of Trump's performance as president among second-generation Americans.
- Exposure to Trump's anti-immigration rhetoric will lead to lower approval of Trump's performance as president among conservative second-generation Americans.

Experimental Procedures

The experimental procedures and stimuli[4] were the same as described in chapter 5.[5] The 2016 experiment included an online sample of second-generation Americans matched to nationally representative census data for this group. The 2017 experiment had online samples of second-generation Americans and US citizens with both parents born in the United States matched to nationally representative census data for these groups. In both experiments, Trump's anti-immigration rhetoric was assigned to be read by one-third of a sample. The other third read a nonpolitical text about birdwatching, while a third read Trump's rhetoric on trade. In the first experiment in 2016, I asked participants post-treatment about their reactions to the texts and their party identification. The second experiment was done in 2017 after Trump became president. It featured the same stimuli but asked

---

4. Again, these randomly assigned stimuli were as follows. For *Trump-immigration*, Donald Trump is the leading candidate for the Republican Party's nomination for President. He opposes illegal immigration and wants to build a wall to keep out those coming in illegally from Mexico. He says that illegal immigrants commit crimes and take jobs away from Americans. For *Trump-trade*, Donald Trump is the leading candidate for the Republican Party's nomination for President. He is opposed to current international free trade deals and wants to scrap these deals or renegotiate them. He says that the countries in these deals commit currency manipulation against the United States dollar and take jobs away from Americans. For the *Control*, the text was "Birdwatching, or birding, is a form of wildlife observation in which the observation of birds is a recreational activity. It can be done with the naked eye, through a visual enhancement device like binoculars and telescopes, or by listening for bird sounds. This hobby has become very popular recently" (from Wikipedia).

5. Participants were recruited to join an online poll by Qualtrics if they were US citizens with at least one foreign-born parent. Qualtrics recruited the sample from a group of five million Americans who had signed up to take surveys for money, and they were paid for this completion. The sample was then constructed to match the proportions of second-generation Americans in the 2010 Census regarding age, income, education, gender, and the percentage of Asian, Hispanic, or black individuals. Appendix table A1 shows that this sample matches census data for second-generation Americans for these measures. While my focus is on the causal inference arising from the experimental method, this sample is broad, geographically diverse, and reasonably representative of second-generation Americans, with the obvious caveats about the nature of who is online and willing to answer survey questions for a cash incentive.

instead about participants' approval of Trump and support for his ideas on immigration. In the 2017 experiment, there was also a pretreatment question about linked fate with immigrants.

Crucially, these survey experiments allow causal inference because of the random assignment and generalizability based on using a matched representative sample of second-generation Americans. After answering some basic demographic and political questions, participants were randomly assigned to read two samples of Trump rhetoric (anti-immigrant or focused on trade) and then answer questions about what they read (see appendix for specific stimuli and wording). The rhetoric was based on the types of comments that Trump typically tweets. They featured insulting and provocative elements, but they were not unusual for him and would be well known to anyone who has followed him on Twitter. They were neither the most extreme nor the most insulting examples of anti-immigration rhetoric, but rather typical of everyday rhetoric from Trump and commonly voiced by members of his wing of the Republican Party. This is important because the experimental stimuli cannot be uncharacteristically strong; otherwise, they would produce results that are not manifested under normal conditions. This type of anti-immigration rhetoric has been a daily occurrence in America's political discourse during the last decade or so.[6]

The two dependent variables are party identification and presidential approval of Trump. In both experiments, party identification was measured with a question that asks, "What political party do you typically support? Democratic (1), Republican (2), Not any party (3), Some other party (4)." Also, in both experiments, presidential approval was asked using the traditional Gallup wording for presidential approval, "Do you approve or disapprove of the way Donald J. Trump is handling his job as President? Approve, No opinion, Disapprove." These variables are analyzed below in the results section.

---

6. It is important to note that due to the experimental setup with unit homogeneity, the focus is on the difference between the randomly assigned stimuli; any pretreatment variables such as ethnicity will be evenly split between treatment conditions. Whether the experimental procedures produced unit homogeneity can be checked by examining the mean difference between the two treatment conditions on several significant variables measured before treatment. Appendix table A2 shows that no statistically significant differences existed between treatment conditions for many vital variables. The groups did not differ concerning age, gender, education, income, or race/ethnicity (i.e., being Asian or Hispanic). Consequently, any difference between the treatment groups can be assumed to be causally related to exposure to the different stimuli.

Experimental Results

I found support for all five of my predictions, but the results were statistically significant for only four. The prediction that did not meet reach significance was the impact of Trump rhetoric on conservative second-generation Americans' identification with the Republican Party; however, the coefficient was in the expected direction. Detailed results are described in the following sections.

Impact of Trump Rhetoric on Republican Party Identification by Second-Generation Americans

Figure 19 shows results from the 2016 experiment that the participants were less likely to identify as Republican after reading Trump's anti-immigration rhetoric. The mean Republican Party identification for the group exposed to anti-immigration rhetoric was 14% versus 25% for the control group ($\beta = -0.1185$; $p = 0.0393$), or a difference of about a quarter of a standard deviation. This finding is the main result of this chapter, and it shows that the crucial variable of partisan identification is influenced by anti-immigration rhetoric. Since party identification is crucial in political behavior, this finding has profound consequences for the future of American politics. It shows that base mobilization strategies also have a flip side that can negatively affect a political party in the long term.

Table 9 shows a probit regression model for the influence of assignment to treatment on Republican Party identification. This more sophisticated modeling tool revealed a statistically significant effect. Trump's rhetoric may provide a short-term boost for the Republican Party in mobilizing base voters, but in the long term it may have a negative impact by repelling second-generation Americans away from the Republican Party. The impact extends beyond Trump himself to the Republican Party in general because Trump is the party's de facto leader. Although Trump will not lead the Republican Party indefinitely, it has embraced anti-immigration rhetoric from several politicians—such as former Colorado representative Tom Tancredo or Representative Steve King of Iowa—for a long time, and is probably permanently associated with it in the minds of many voters.

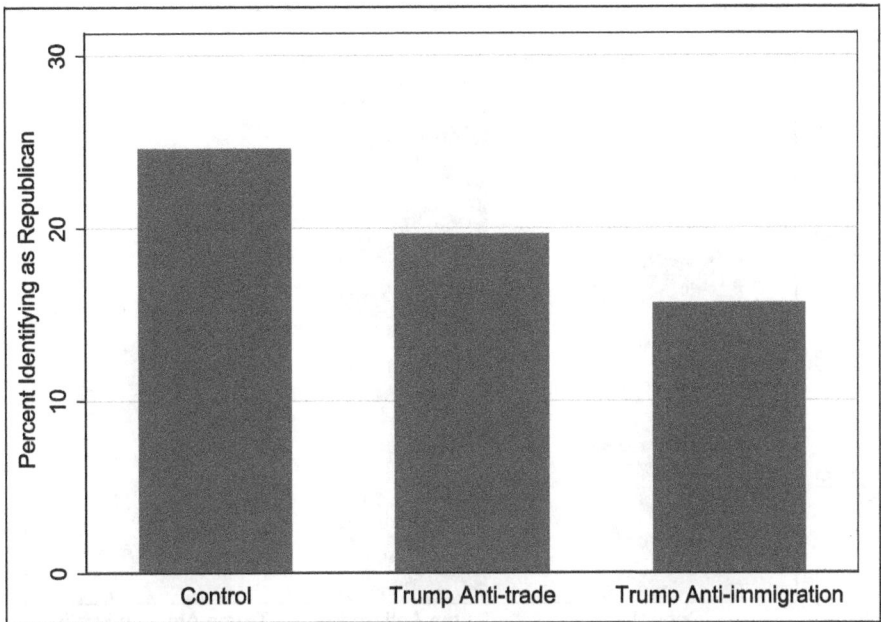

Fig. 19. The level of Republican Party identification after exposure to the treatment conditions.

TABLE 9. Effect of Exposure to Trump Rhetoric on Identification with the Republican Party

	Coef.	S.E.
Trump anti-immigration	−0.343*	0.166
Trump antitrade	−0.249	0.168
Intercept	−0.680***	0.110
N	439	
χ^2	4.668	

Note: Cells represent unstandardized coefficients and standard errors of a probit regression model for the influence of assignment to treatment on Republican Party identification versus the control condition. The sample includes individuals whose parents were both born outside the United States, and it is matched to census data for these groups in the United States in terms of age, education, income, and gender.
*$p < 0.05$, **$p < 0.01$, ***$p < 0.001$

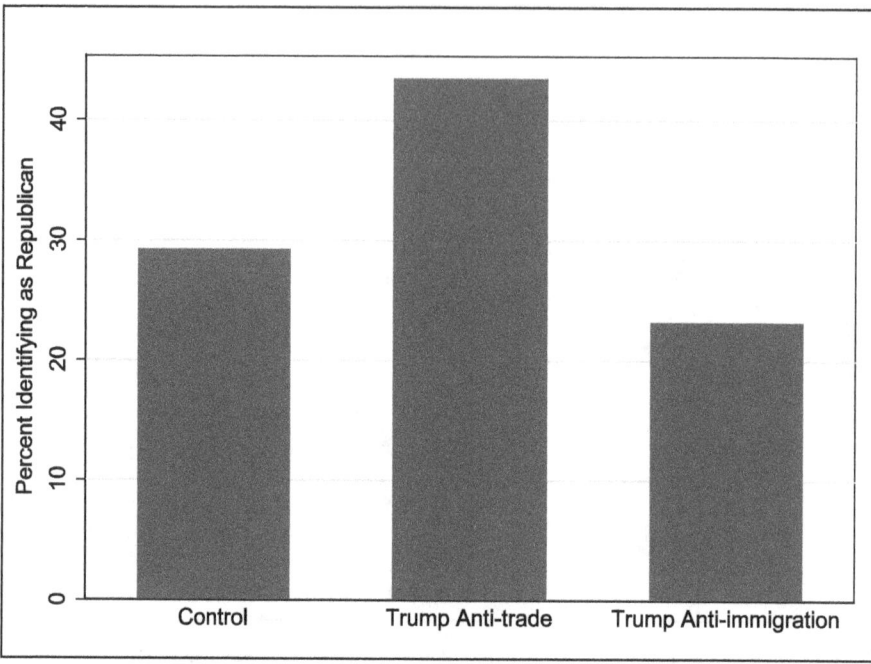

Fig. 20. The level of Republican Party identification after exposure to the treatment conditions for conservative second-generation Americans.

Impact of Trump Rhetoric on Republican Party Identification by Conservative Second-Generation Americans

Conservative second-generation Americans had a lower level of expressed support for the Republican Party, but the difference was not statistically significant. Figure 20 shows a 4 percentage point drop in Republican Party identification for conservative second-generation Americans associated with the treatment. Because the effect was not statistically significant, it is difficult to judge whether the reduction is due to exposure, statistical power issues because the low sample size may preclude accurate measurement, or a simple lack of effect.

Results by Ethnicity of Participant

Trump often refers explicitly to Latinos when he comments on immigration, and they are directly mentioned by Huntington (2004) as being particularly prominent in discussions about immigration. Given the focus on

TABLE 10. Effect of Exposure to Trump Rhetoric for Hispanic Americans on Identification with the Republican Party

	Coef.	S.E.
Hispanic × Trump-imm	0.591	0.573
Hispanic × Trump-trade	0.300	0.514
Hispanic	0.204	0.294
Trump anti-immigration	−1.234*	0.508
Trump anti-trade	−0.807	0.441
Intercept	−0.552*	0.238
N	243	
χ^2	18.248**	

Note: Cells represent unstandardized coefficients and standard errors of a probit regression model for the influence of assignment to treatment on Republican Party identification versus the control condition for Hispanic Americans. The sample includes individuals whose parents were both born outside the United States, and it is matched to census data for these groups in the United States in terms of age, education, income, and gender.

*$p < 0.05$, **$p < 0.01$, ***$p < 0.001$

this subpopulation in anti-immigration rhetoric within American politics, I examine whether the rhetoric has a more significant impact on Latinos. Latinos constituted 68% of the sample, which enabled investigating this possibility. Table 10 shows interaction effects between random assignment to the anti-incorporation treatment and being Hispanic American. No significant effects for being Hispanic and assignment to treatment were apparent across all dependent variables. This outcome suggests that the rhetoric did not have a unique impact on this subpopulation; the effects of exposure were similar for all second-generation Americans in this sample.

Another large immigrant group that Trump sometimes refers to is Asian Americans. Table 11 shows interaction effects between the treatments and being Asian American. No significant effects of being Asian American and assignment to treatment were apparent across all dependent variables. This outcome suggests that the two subpopulations were similar concerning the effect of anti-immigration rhetoric, and their beliefs on matters of incorporation were also similar. As was stated in chapter 5, I will investigate the impact of the Trump era on different ethnic groups within these populations in chapter 7.

Impact of Trump Rhetoric on Approval of Trump by Second-Generation Americans

With regard to the level of participants' approval of Trump, I examined the results from the 2017 experiment after exposure to the treatment conditions. Figure 21 shows that both groups exhibited a similar pattern in the

TABLE 11. Effect of Exposure to Trump Rhetoric for Asian Americans on Identification with the Republican Party

	Coef.	S.E.
Asian American × Trump-imm	−0.511	0.641
Asian American × Trump-trade	0.186	0.559
Asian American	0.125	0.355
Trump anti-immigration	−0.671**	0.247
Trump anti-trade	−0.603*	0.251
Intercept	−0.444**	0.155
N	243	
χ^2	14.297*	

Note: Cells represent unstandardized coefficients and standard errors of a probit regression model for the influence of assignment to treatment on Republican Party identification versus the control condition for Asian Americans. The sample includes individuals whose parents were both born outside the United States, and it is matched to census data for these groups in the United States in terms of age, education, income, and gender.

*$p < 0.05$, **$p < 0.01$, ***$p < 0.001$

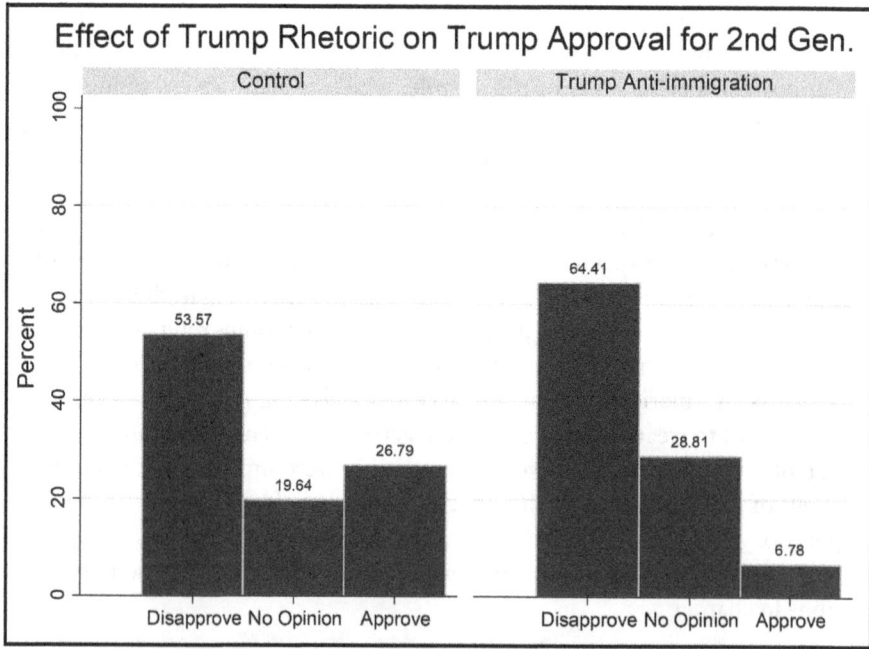

Fig. 21. The difference in Trump approval after exposure to experimental stimuli for second-generation Americans.

TABLE 12. Effect of Exposure to Trump Rhetoric on Trump Approval

	2nd Gen.	S.E.	Not 2nd Gen.	S.E.
Approve of Trump				
Trump anti-immigration	−1.092**	0.422	−0.218	0.339
Trump antitrade	−0.525	0.374	0.311	0.328
Intercept	−0.567*	0.254	−0.516*	0.223
No opinion of Trump				
Trump anti-immigration	0.107	0.362	−0.081	0.384
Trump antitrade	−0.541	0.400	−0.091	0.401
Intercept	−0.793**	0.269	−1.048***	0.257
N	170		182	
χ^2	11.360*		2.815	

Note: Cells represent unstandardized coefficients and standard errors of multinomial probit regression models for the influence of assignment to treatment for Trump approval versus the control condition. The base category is disapproval of Trump. Not 2nd Gen. includes individuals whose parents were both born in the United States, while 2nd Gen. includes individuals whose parents were both born outside the United States. Both samples are matched to census data for these groups in the United States in terms of age, education, income and gender.
*$p < 0.05$, **$p < 0.01$, ***$p < 0.001$

distribution of responses, but the group exposed to the anti-immigration rhetoric was more likely to disapprove of Trump. The mean Trump approval for the group exposed to anti-immigration rhetoric was 6% versus 26% for the control group (β = −0.1391; p = 0.0308), or a difference of about a quarter of a standard deviation. This finding shows that the impact of anti-immigration rhetoric was not merely limited to Republican Party identification but also extended to the president's approval.

A pairwise correlation between these variables is not optimal for analyzing these data because Trump's approval is best thought of as a categorical variable due to the way the question was asked, which was based on a Gallup survey question. A multinomial probit is a superior modeling strategy for categorical variables. Table 12 shows a multinomial probit regression model result, which revealed a statistically significant effect from exposure to Trump's anti-immigration rhetoric, but not to his antitrade rhetoric. This outcome shows that the causal mechanism was through exposure to the anti-immigration rhetoric because exposure to Trump's antitrade rhetoric—which conveys his personality, personal characteristics, and anti-globalism slant—did not have a statistically significant effect.

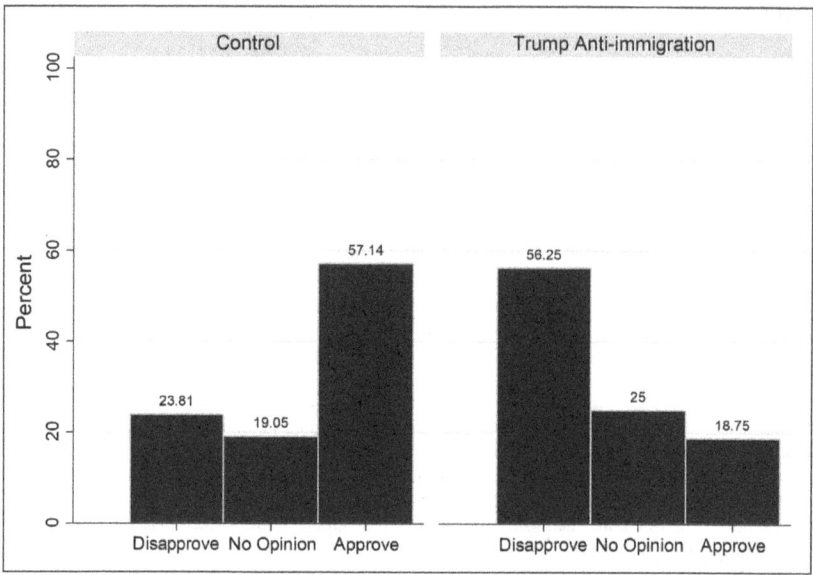

Fig. 22. The difference in Trump approval after exposure to experimental stimuli for conservative second-generation Americans.

Impact of Trump Rhetoric on Trump Approval by Conservative Second-Generation Americans

I next tested the approval of Trump by conservative second-generation Americans in the 2017 experiment. Figure 22 shows a large effect of exposure to anti-immigration rhetoric of around 40 percentage points. The mean approval of Trump for the group exposed to anti-immigration rhetoric was 18% versus 57% for the control group[7] ($\beta = -0.2422$; $p = 0.0169$),

---

7. Why is the control group so supportive of Trump at 57% if his rhetoric is perceived negatively? The control group in figure 22 has had a lot of exposure to Trump's rhetoric, just like all Americans have, but this experiment measures the treatment effect. It shows that brief exposure to a small amount of Trump's rhetoric has a negative effect. Even though both groups have had prior exposure, the difference between the randomly assigned treatment and control groups is the effect of Trump's rhetoric. Many factors affect public opinion toward a president or a political party. Trump's rhetoric is, of course, just one of many factors. This experiment tries to isolate the effect of Trump's rhetoric by measuring the difference between exposure and nonexposure. Many long-term factors affect party identification and opinions toward Trump, who has been in the American media for decades, and all of those prior opinions and former stimuli are brought into the experiment by both the treatment and control groups. However, the most critical factor in the experiment is not the control group's level but the difference between the control and treatment groups.

TABLE 13. Effect of Exposure to Trump Rhetoric on Trump Approval for Conservatives

	2nd Gen.	S.E.	Not 2nd Gen.	S.E.
Approve of Trump				
Trump anti-immigration	−1.584*	0.659	−0.530	0.472
Trump antitrade	−0.826	0.608	0.155	0.477
Intercept	0.713	0.422	0.344	0.344
No opinion of Trump				
Trump anti-immigration	−0.502	0.680	0.023	0.584
Trump antitrade	−0.866	0.731	0.016	0.627
Intercept	−0.161	0.482	−0.857	0.447
N	54		91	
χ^2	6.730		2.959	

Note: Cells represent unstandardized coefficients and standard errors of multinomial probit regression models for the influence of assignment to treatment for Trump approval versus the control condition. The base category is disapproval of Trump. Not 2nd Gen. includes individuals whose parents were both born in the United States, while 2nd Gen. includes individuals whose parents were both born outside the United States. Both samples are matched to census data for these groups in the United States in terms of age, education, income, and gender. Limited to those who rate themselves as at least slightly conservative on a standard 7-point ideology scale.
*$p < 0.05$, **$p < 0.01$, ***$p < 0.001$

or a difference of about a half of a standard deviation. Interestingly, most conservatives in the control condition supported Trump, but the majority of those with exposure to his anti-immigration rhetoric did not support him. This finding shows that reminding the children of immigrants about Trump's anti-immigrant positions has a large effect on their level of support for him, even though they may have been strongly inclined to support him based on other ideological positions.

The multinomial logit model shown in table 13 confirms the pairwise correlations found in figure 22. Individuals in the anti-immigration rhetoric condition were much less likely to approve of Trump.

Replication of Results with 2016 ANES Survey Data

As I did in chapter 5, I will now replicate the experimental results with nationally representative survey data, this time from 1952–2020. As stated, the advantage of this approach is that it shows that the basic correlations replicate in survey data outside of the experimental conditions. Demonstrating the results' external validity allows for additional confidence that these results are not a function of the experimental conditions. Again, by themselves, these results would only establish correlation and not causation. However, the causal relationship between Trump's rhetoric and second-generation American attitudes has been established through the experimental results earlier in this chapter.

The *Trump on ballot* variable is coded (1) if the survey was taken in a year when Trump was on the ballot—that is, the 2016 and 2020 elections—and (0) if Trump was not on the ballot. This becomes an indicator variable of a survey conducted in a communication environment where anti-immigration rhetoric is profoundly common. Chapter 4 shows that these years had a higher level of anti-immigration rhetoric than earlier times due to Trump. The Trump on ballot variable interacts with a dichotomous variable of whether the respondent is a second-generation American to determine the unique impact on second-generation Americans in the Trump era, on voting for a Republican presidential candidate and attitudes toward the Republican Party.

In table 14, the Presidential Vote model is a logistic regression model for determinants of voting for a Republican presidential candidate from 1952 to 2020. The dependent variable is two-party vote share, with nonvoters and third-party voters excluded from the analysis. The dependent variable has a Republican vote for president coded (1), and a Democratic vote for President coded (0). The party identification model is an ordered logistic regression model for determinants of party identification, also from 1952 to 2020. The dependent variable is a standard seven-part Likert scale, coded from extremely Democratic (1) to extremely Republican (7).

It is important to consider how over time trends may affect these results. There is a long-term trend of loss of support for the Republican Party among second-generation Americans, and the results could be a function of more longer-term phenomena outside of Trump's rhetoric. If so, the statistical analysis that presents over time survey data does not account for this long-term trend. The most effective way is to control for the time trend in a regression model. Because these are yearly surveys, by including the year that the survey was taken as a regressor in the regression model, it acts as a way to control trends expressed through time. Table 14 shows that even when controlling for over time trends (the *Year of election* variable), Trump being on the ballot had a unique negative effect on support for the Republican Party and Republican presidential nominees from second-generation Americans. This implies that Trump's impact is separate from the simultaneously occurring negative trends controlled by the "year" variable.

TABLE 14. Determinants of Republican Presidential Vote and Party Identification, 1952–2020

Variable	Presidential Vote	S.E.	Party ID	S.E.
Second generation × Trump on ballot	−0.086*	0.041	−0.132***	0.028
Second generation	−0.363***	0.037	−0.173***	0.020
Trump on ballot	0.059	0.055	0.075	0.042
Black	−1.698***	0.092	−0.933***	0.055
Education	0.036	0.031	0.052**	0.017
Age	0.006***	0.001	0.000	0.001
Male	0.124***	0.023	0.100***	0.024
Income	−0.004	0.005	0.004	0.006
Year of election	−0.007**	0.002	0.000	0.001
Intercept	13.121**	4.915		
Cut point 1			−0.072	1.859
Cut point 2			0.515	1.847
Cut point 3			0.840	1.845
Cut point 4			1.166	1.837
Cut point 5			1.479	1.834
Cut point 6			1.975	1.823
N	26,505		52,872	
Log likelihood	−16542.441		−98921.935	

Note: Cells in the Presidential Vote model represent unstandardized coefficients and standard errors for logistic regression models for determinants of voting for a Republican presidential candidate from 1952 in 2020. The dependent variable is two-party vote share, with nonvoters and third-party voters excluded from the analysis. The dependent variable has a Republican vote for president coded (1), and a Democratic vote for president coded (0). Cells in the party identification model represent unstandardized coefficients and standard errors for ordered logistic regression models for determinants of party identification from 1952 in 2020. The dependent variable is a standard seven-part Likert scale, coded from extremely Democratic (1) to extremely Republican (7).

+$p < .10$, *$p < .05$, **$p < .01$, ***$p < .001$

As shown in table 14, second-generation Americans were less likely to vote for a Republican nominee when Trump is on the ballot in 2016 and 2020, with a *p*-value of less than .000. Second-generation Americans voted 42% on average for the Republican presidential nominee from 1952 to 2012. However, in the two elections with Trump on the ballot, only 31% voted for Trump in 2016 and 2020. Comparing before and after the Trump era, second-generation Americans are about 10 percentage points lower in supporting Trump than other Republican candidates. This logistic regression model includes the time trend, so it is not merely a function of less Republican support over time. There was something specific about Trump that lowered his voting rates. Note that the interaction term includes non-

TABLE 15. Determinants of Voting for Trump in 2020

Variable	1	S.E.	2	S.E.
Second generation	−1.016***	0.140	−0.764***	0.187
Hispanic			−1.179***	0.207
Asian			−0.162	0.287
Black			−2.897***	0.355
Education			−0.337***	0.042
Age			0.012***	0.003
Male			0.149	0.084
Income			0.005	0.008
Intercept	−0.062	0.040	0.506*	0.215
N	5,381		4,945	
χ^2	52.723***		225.232***	

Note: Cells represent unstandardized coefficients and standard errors for logistic regression models for determinants of voting for Trump in 2020. The dependent variable is two-party vote share, with nonvoters and third-party voters excluded from the analysis. The dependent variable has a Trump voter coded (1), and a Biden voter coded (0).
+$p < .10$, *$p < .05$, **$p < .01$, ***$p < .001$

TABLE 16. Determinants of Voting for Party Identification in 2020

Variable	1	S.E.	2	S.E.
Second generation	−0.531***	0.083	−0.397***	0.108
Hispanic			−0.557***	0.109
Asian			−0.256	0.187
Black			−1.990***	0.119
Education			−0.186***	0.031
Age			0.003	0.002
Male			0.225***	0.062
Income			0.006	0.005
Cut point 1	−1.360***	0.045	−1.950***	0.143
Cut point 2	−0.799***	0.039	−1.323***	0.140
Cut point 3	−0.317***	0.037	−0.784***	0.139
Cut point 4	0.241***	0.036	−0.200	0.139
Cut point 5	0.695***	0.038	0.287*	0.140
Cut point 6	1.267***	0.042	0.891***	0.141
N	6,956		6,360	
χ^2	40.839***		378.877***	

Note: Cells represent unstandardized coefficients and standard errors for ordered logistic regression models for determinants of party identification in 2020. The dependent variable is a standard seven-part Likert scale, coded from extremely Democratic (1) to extremely Republican (7).
+$p < .10$, *$p < .05$, **$p < .01$, ***$p < .001$

TABLE 17. Determinants of Voting for Trump in 2020 by Second-Generation Americans

Variable	q	S.E.	2	S.E.	3	S.E.
Hispanic	−0.765**	0.233	−0.595*	0.263	−0.844*	0.350
Black	−2.962**	1.027	−2.814**	1.032	−2.625*	1.087
Asian	−0.399	0.226	−0.217	0.248	−0.542	0.337
Ideology					1.247***	0.128
Age			0.018**	0.006	0.001	0.008
Income			0.004	0.016	0.032	0.023
Education			−0.105	0.081	−0.016	0.122
Male			0.048	0.202	0.101	0.270
Intercept	−0.439**	0.145	−1.192*	0.544	−6.057***	0.921
N	558.000		512.000		444.000	
χ^2	26.643***		35.884***		186.202***	

Note: Cells represent unstandardized coefficients and standard errors for logistic regression models for determinants of voting for Trump in 2020 for second-generation Americans. The dependent variable is two-party vote share, with nonvoters and third party voters excluded from the analysis. The dependent variable has a Trump vote for president coded (1), and a Biden vote for president coded (0).

+p < .10, *p < .05, **p < .01, ***p < .001

second-generation Americans, so this is not a part of a long-term trend in America, but something specific to being second-generation American when Trump was a candidate.

Also shown in table 14, second-generation Americans had less identification with the Republican Party when Trump was on the ballot in 2016 and 2020, with a *p*-value of less than .000. Thus, second-generation Americans did vote less often for presidential nominees and identified with the Republican Party less in the Trump era, which replicates the primary findings of the survey experiment results.

There were several reports that counties with large Latino or Asian populations supported Trump at a greater level in 2020 (see, e.g., Cai and Fessenden 2020). While this may be true at the aggregate for these counties, it is vital to test the specific data on second-generation Americans to determine if these results negate the findings of the experiments. In tables 15 and 16, I use new survey data from the 2020 election to show that second-generation Americans are less likely to vote for Trump even after controlling for other relevant variables. Table 15 is a logistic regression model that shows that second-generation Americans are less likely to vote for Donald Trump in the 2020 presidential election. Table 16 is an ordered logistic regression model that shows that second-generation Americans are less likely to have a Republican Party identification. Thus, the primary results found in the experiment are not contradicted by survey data on voting for second-generation Americans in 2020.

Another approach to answering whether Hispanics or Asian Americans were more likely to vote for Trump in the 2020 election is to take survey data from the 2020 election and create a regression model using only second-generation American respondents. Table 17 uses second-generation Americans from the 2020 ANES survey and regresses social and economic variables on two-party vote share, including ethnicity. The entire sample shown in table 17 are second-generation Americans. The table lists unstandardized coefficients and standard errors for logistic regression models for determinants of voting for Trump in 2020 for second-generation Americans. The dependent variable is two-party vote share, with nonvoters and third-party voters excluded from the analysis. The dependent variable has a Trump vote for president coded (1) and a Biden vote for president coded (0).

Table 17 shows that Hispanics who are second-generation Americans show less propensity in all three models to vote for Trump in 2020. Asian Americans are not significant, which implies that they are not different from other ethnic groups in the likelihood that they will vote for Trump or not. Interestingly, most of the other socioeconomic variables are not statistically significant, except age and ideology. In sum, tables 15, 16, and 17 show the results are similar in the 2020 election as they were in the 2016 election. Second-generation Americans are less likely to vote for Trump, which augments the experimental evidence, which shows that they are repulsed explicitly by his anti-immigration rhetoric.

Conclusion

To uncover the impact of anti-immigration rhetoric on party identification and presidential approval, I conducted two experiments on online samples in 2016 and 2017 matched to nationally representative census data for these groups. I replicated the primary finding with ANES survey data from 1952 to 2020. The results show that second-generation Americans were less likely to support the Republican Party after exposure to Trump's anti-immigration rhetoric, and they were disproportionately less likely to approve of the president after exposure to his rhetoric. Party identification and presidential approval were measured after exposure to the treatment conditions, after reading about Trump's ideas on immigration or trade, or a control condition based on a nonpolitical text about birdwatching. Some evidence extended to conservative second-generation Americans, which is fascinating because they should support Trump and the Republican Party if they strictly voted based on their ideological beliefs.

These results greatly inform us about the unsettled nature of partisan attachment among second-generation Americans. Many scholars emphasize how the pressure on immigrants and their descendants to incorporate should match their party identification to the microenvironment in which they live. Many scholars of immigration have assumed that second-generation immigrants would often become Republican because they often reside in states such as Texas or Arizona that are predominantly Republican. However, the current study shows that many US-born children of immigrants are offended by the national-level rhetoric, which can influence partisan identification.

The causality shown by the experimental method combined with the external validity of a matched representative sample makes the results convincing. The viewpoints of minority populations are often obtained from a small subset of a nationally representative sample. By targeting this subpopulation, I was able to conduct a more valid assessment of their beliefs. Again, as stated in chapter 5, these experimental research procedures do not allow us to examine these effects over time, and they may dissipate quickly or perhaps even gain in importance. Without longitudinal data, I cannot determine the long-term effects of exposure to Trump's rhetoric. However, table 14 shows that the Trump era had 10 percentage points less voting for the Republican presidential nominee and lower Republican party identification by second-generation Americans.

In the next chapter, I look at how the ethnicity of second-generation Americans differentiates these results.

References

Andersen, Kristi. 2008. "In Whose Interest? Political Parties, Context, and the Incorporation of Immigrants." In *New Race Politics in America: Understanding Minority and Immigrant Politics*, edited by Jane Junn and Kerry L. Haynie. Cambridge: Cambridge University Press.

Berelson, Bernard R., Paul F. Lazarsfeld, and William N. McPhee. 1954. *Voting*. Chicago: University of Chicago Press.

Cai, Weiyi, and Ford Fessenden. 2020. "Immigrant Neighborhoods Shifted Red as the Country Chose Blue." *New York Times*. December 21. https://www.nytimes.com/interactive/2020/12/20/us/politics/election-hispanics-asians-voting.html

Campbell, Angus, Philip E. Converse, Warren E. Miller, and Donald E. Stokes. 1960. *The American Voter*. New York: John Wiley & Sons.

Clarke, Harold, and Marianne Stewart. 1998. "The Decline of Parties in the Minds of Citizens." *Annual Review of Political Science* 1:357–78.

Gallup. 2021. "Presidential Approval Ratings—Gallup Historical Statistics and

Trends." Gallup.com. August 12. https://news.gallup.com/poll/116677/presidential-approval-ratings-gallup-historical-statistics-trends.aspx

Hajnal, Zoltan, and Taeku Lee. 2011. *Why Americans Don't Join the Party: Race, Immigration, and the Failure (of Political Parties) to Engage the Electorate.* Princeton: Princeton University Press.

Hero, Rodney. 1992. *Latinos and the US Political System: Two-Tiered Pluralism.* Philadelphia: Temple University Press.

Huntington, Samuel. 2004. *Who Are We? The Challenges to America's National Identity.* New York: Simon & Shuster.

Jennings, M. Kent, and Richard G. Niemi. 1974. *The Political Character of Adolescence.* Princeton: Princeton University Press.

Jennings, M. Kent., and Richard G. Niemi. 1981. *Generations and Politics: A Panel Study of Young Adults and Their Parents.* Princeton: Princeton University Press.

Jerit, Jennifer, and Jason Barabas. 2012. "Partisan Perceptual Bias and the Information Environment." *Journal of Politics* 74 (3): 672–84.

Kim, Thomas P. 2007. *The Racial Logic of Politics: Asian Americans and Party Competition.* Philadelphia: Temple University Press.

Lee, Taeku. 2008a. "Race, Immigration, and the Identity-to-Politics Link." *Annual Review of Political Science* 11:457–78.

Lee, Taeku. 2008b. "From Shared Demographic Categories to Common Political Destinies? Immigration and the Link from Racial Identity to Group Politics." *DuBois Review* 4:433–56.

Massey, Douglas, and Magaly Sánchez. 2010. *Brokered Boundaries: Creating Immigrant Identity in Anti-Immigrant Times.* New York: Russell Sage Foundation.

McPherson, Miller, Lynn Smith-Lovin, and James M. Cook. 2001. "Birds of a Feather: Homophily in Social Networks." *Annual Review of Sociology* 27:415–44.

Rove, Karl. 2013. "Immigration Reform and the Hispanic Vote." *Wall Street Journal*, June 5.

Sessions, Jeff. 2017. "A Memo For Republican Members from Sen. Jeff Sessions, Immigration Handbook for the New Republican Majority; Quote from Subcommittee Hearing on 'The Impact of High Levels of Immigration on US Workers.'" Memo.

Taber, Charles S., and Milton Lodge. 2006. "Motivated Skepticism in the Evaluation of Political Beliefs." *American Journal of Political Science* 50 (3): 755–69.

Wong, Janelle. 2008. *Democracy's Promise: Immigrants and American Civic Institutions.* Ann Arbor: University of Michigan Press.

Wong, Janelle, S. Karthick Ramakrishnan, Taeku Lee, and Jane Junn. 2011. *Asian American Political Participation: Emerging Constituents and Their Political Identities.* New York: Russell Sage Foundation.

CHAPTER 7

Disaggregating the Attitudes of Second-Generation Americans

So far, I have investigated the impact of anti-immigration rhetoric on second-generation Americans broadly. This chapter disaggregates those results by examining available data on second-generation Americans' attitudes based on their parents' birth country. Pan-ethnic groupings such as Asian Americans, Hispanics, and Latinos are generalized labels that do not fully account for these second-generation Americans' lived experiences. Survey data show that second-generation Americans often categorize themselves more narrowly, using terms such as Korean American or Dominican rather than pan-ethnic labels. It is essential to delve into these distinctions to determine the full impact of anti-immigration rhetoric on second-generation Americans. Although a statistically significant difference in the treatment effect between Latinos and Asian Americans was not observed in the previous chapters, that may have been due to the low number of respondents. I could not analyze differences between Salvadoran Americans and Cuban Americans, for example, yet that does not preclude the existence of distinctions between these subgroups.

It has long been known, for example, that Cuban Americans are more politically conservative and more likely than other Latinos to vote for Republicans. This tendency is attributed to Fidel Castro's regime's abusive nature and the tough anticommunist stance of the Republican Party from the 1964 presidential campaign of Barry Goldwater through President Ronald Reagan's administration into the late 1980s. Some scholars even describe Cuban Americans as single-issue voters, with anticommunism being the issue (Garcia 1996). The Republican Party during the Cold War owned the issue of anticommunism and thus established a stronghold within this group (Eckstein 2009). Similarly, for Vietnamese Americans, communism remains a critical issue today because an autocratic communist regime still rules Vietnam. In a process very similar to that of Cuban Americans, Vietnamese Americans were attracted to the Republican Party's staunch anticommunism, particularly under Reagan (Le and Su 2018).

We can expect then that party identification and conservative ideology will color the impact of anti-immigration rhetoric coming from the party that one supports. An extensive literature exists on motivated reasoning based on partisanship (Lodge and Taber 2013). Motivated partisan reasoning could diminish negative interpretations of Donald Trump's harsh rhetoric because Cuban Americans and Vietnamese Americans may have a more positive view of Republican candidates due to the long-standing identification of these two groups with the Republican Party.

Notably, my theory included a lemma that these groups did not need long-standing partisan identification for Trump's rhetoric to be impactful. However, there is evidence of significant prior socialization within America's party system for Cuban Americans and Vietnamese Americans. Therefore, the theory would predict that these groups would be less affected by Trump's rhetoric. I expect that Cuban Americans and Vietnamese Americans had a more positive view of the Republican Party and Donald Trump in 2016 and 2017, even though the rhetoric of both has been shown in chapter 4 to be anti-immigrant.

Additionally, since Trump's rhetoric specifically targets Mexico and immigration from Mexico—and this rhetoric is his harshest—I expect Mexican Americans to be disproportionately affected by Trump's rhetoric. I would expect that the data from 2016 and 2017 would show that Trump's relationship with second-generation Mexican Americans was the least positive relative to other second-generation groups.

Using three new datasets collected either during the 2016 election or afterward, I analyzed important subgroups among Latinos and Asian Americans. Two of these three datasets specifically target large samples from subethnic groups within the more prominent pan-ethnic labels. Pew Research did a survey in 2017 that analyzed the attitudes of Latinos toward Trump. This sample has two features that were important for the research in this chapter. First, it oversampled second-generation Americans. Secondly, it included targeted samples for Mexican Americans, Cuban Americans, and Salvadoran Americans and data on several other Latino subgroups due to its large size. These data will allow us to ascertain the impact of Trump on these subgroups of Latinos.

Similarly, the National Asian American Survey was conducted just after the 2016 presidential election and provided detailed data on several significant subgroups based on parental home country (Ramakrishnan et al. 2018). Importantly, this survey includes both South Asian and East Asian Americans. I augment these surveys with additional data from the ANES. Before examining the data, it is essential to see how the theory predicts diminished impact from Trump's rhetoric for Cuban Americans and Vietnamese Americans and an attenuated impact for Mexican Americans. It is important to note that this chapter uses datasets that have different questions from the questions posed in prior chapters, such as chapter 4. This chapter tries to examine holistically the effect of Trump's rhetoric on the attitudes of second-generation Americans by ethnic subgroups, and the only data that has enough in the sample to analyze these subgroups does not have the exact same questions as was used in the experiments. I start by analyzing different ethnic subgroups of second-generation Latinos' attitudes toward Trump and the Republican Party in the Trump era.

Attitudes of Second-Generation Latinos, by Parental Home Country

Using data from the Pew study from 2017, we can analyze second-generation Latinos' attitudes toward Trump and the Republican Party. Figure 23 shows the opinion about the situation of Latinos in America since Trump became president. Opinions are divided by subgroupings within the second-generation category for Latinos. The data have a large oversample of Latinos that can be broken down by parental birth country, and some findings will repeat throughout the data examined in this chapter.

First, notice that other than Cuban Americans, there is no statistically significant difference between Mexican Americans, Dominican Americans, Salvadoran Americans, Spanish Americans,[1] and other Latinos. This implies that the impact of Trump's presidency on these other subgroupings is similar. It may be that Donald Trump's harsh rhetoric toward the MS13 street gang, which is associated with Salvadoran immigrants, alienated Salvadoran Americans in the same way that his harsh rhetoric against Mexican Americans has. Furthermore, his generally hostile rhetoric toward immi-

---

1. To be clear, Pew had a category for Americans with parental ancestry from Spain, which they term Spanish Americans. I utilize their categorization scheme.

gration from Latin America seems to uniformly influence these groups to perceive their place in American society during his presidency negatively. Moreover, while the figures show slight differences between Spanish and Mexican second-generation Americans, it is essential not to overinterpret these results because the differences are not statistically significant.

The other chief finding is that Cuban Americans are the only subgroup that does not perceive that their situation worsened under Trump in 2017. On average, Cuban Americans feel that their situation in America improved during the first year of Donald Trump's presidency. This outcome suggests that Trump's rhetoric was not as impactful on this group because they had developed schema placing him within America's party system and adapted their views on his presidency through the lens of being identified with the Republican Party. These findings clearly show the importance of distinguishing between second-generation Americans who have long-standing party identifications and those who are less attached to America's party system and have less ingrained partisan identification.

The same survey asked another question about which party has more concern for Latinos. Figure 24 clearly shows a pattern similar to that in figure 23. Mexican Americans, Dominican Americans, Salvadoran Americans, Spanish Americans, and other Latinos feel that the Democratic Party is more likely to be concerned about Latinos. I also find that most Cuban Americans feel that the Republican Party is more likely to be concerned for Latinos in 2017. This is clear evidence that Trump's harsh anti-immigration rhetoric has not altered Cuban Americans' long-standing identification with the Republican Party. Cuban Americans remain loyal Republicans and are not affected by the change in political rhetoric described in chapter 4.

These results have important implications for the future of political incorporation. If changes in beliefs about a group's place in American society delimit willingness to engage with the broader society, it may have down-the-line negative impacts on group members' democratic citizenship. Making Latinos feel as though the Republican Party—including many Americans who vote Republican—does not care for them may alienate these citizens and make them feel unwelcome in their home country.

Figure 25 shows voting in the 2016 election by second-generation Cuban Americans, Mexican Americans, and Salvadoran Americans. Due to many respondents in the other subgroups who did not vote, data from these groups are not included because their number of voters in the sample is minimal. We see that second-generation Cuban Americans are more likely to have voted for Trump than other second-generation subgroups

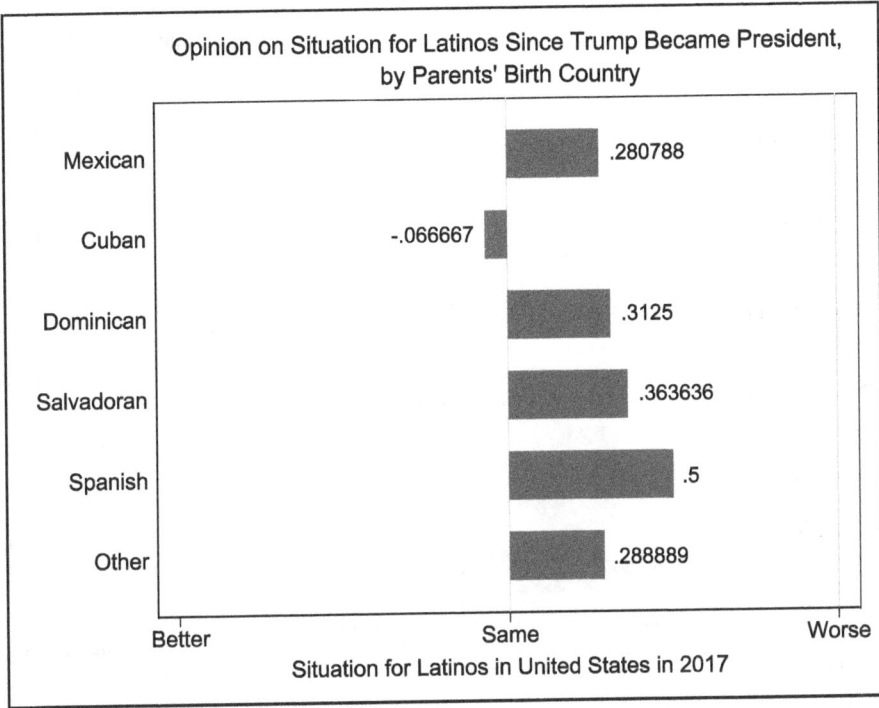

Fig. 23. Second-generation Americans' opinions on changes in Latinos' situation, separated by parental home country.

such as Mexican Americans and Salvadoran Americans. The data show that 40% of Cuban Americans in the sample say they voted for Trump in the 2016 election. Moreover, while we may expect most Cuban Americans to vote for the Republican Party, it is important to remember again that these respondents are second-generation Americans and probably differ in some respects from other generations. Among Salvadoran and Mexican Americans, we see that only around 10% voted for Trump in the 2016 election, which provides strong evidence that these second-generation Americans were resistant to Trump as a candidate.

Thus far, we have not seen any statistically significant differences between second-generation Mexican Americans and other second-generation Latinos, aside from Cuban Americans. One reason may be that the questions were about politics in general and were not specific to Mexican Americans. Figure 26, however, shows that Mexican Americans have a disproportionately robust dislike of Trump compared with other Repub-

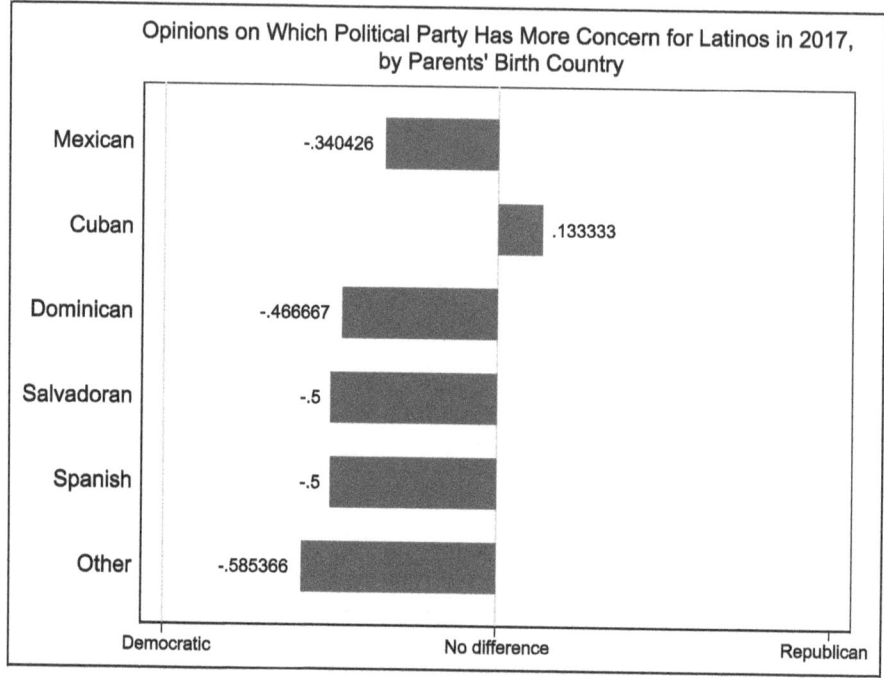

Fig. 24. Second-generation Americans' opinions on which party has more concern for Latinos, separated by parental home country.

lican presidential candidates. The ANES included a thermometer feeling question about presidential candidates for decades. Using these data, we can examine second-generation Mexican Americans' attitudes toward various Republican candidates for the presidency from 1980 until 2000.

Differences might be expected to emerge when the topic specifically addresses immigration from Mexico. Trump's signature issue on immigration was to build a wall at the US border with Mexico to separate the countries. In truth, much of the cross-border immigration over the Rio Grande involves Central Americans who migrate through Mexico on their way to the United States. Nevertheless, because the border is with Mexico and millions of Mexican Americans have ancestors who crossed this border, building a border wall is an issue that speaks directly to this population's family history. In other words, there may be a disproportionate effect with Mexican Americans compared with other Latinos on issues that specifically address immigration from Mexico. No other policy in the Trump era is as salient as is his proposal to "build the wall." It became a defining character-

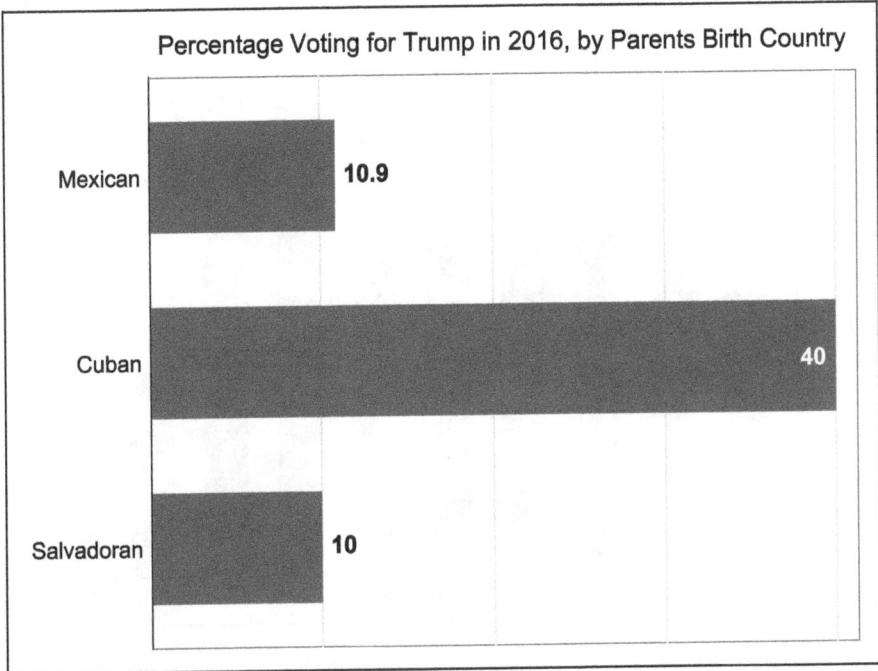

Fig. 25. Second-generation Americans' vote for Trump, separated by parental home country.

istic of his campaign and a crucial symbol of his anti-immigration policies. Of note, the phrase "build the wall" has denigrated into a derogatory slur and is used to taunt Mexican Americans.

The 2016 ANES asked a question about support for Trump's idea to build the wall. This dichotomous question was coded as 1 if the respondent supported building a wall and 0 if they did not. Figure 27 shows the percentage of respondents who gave an affirmative answer in support of Trump's idea to build the wall, and the difference between second-generation Mexican Americans and other second-generation Americans is apparent. Mexican Americans were less likely to express support for building the wall, and the difference was statistically significant. On a scale of 1 (oppose) to 7 (support), second-generation Mexican Americans were strongly opposed to building the wall, whereas other second-generation Americans were only slightly against building the wall. There was around half of a standard deviation difference between these groups in supporting building the wall, which was significant at p-value <.001. This finding

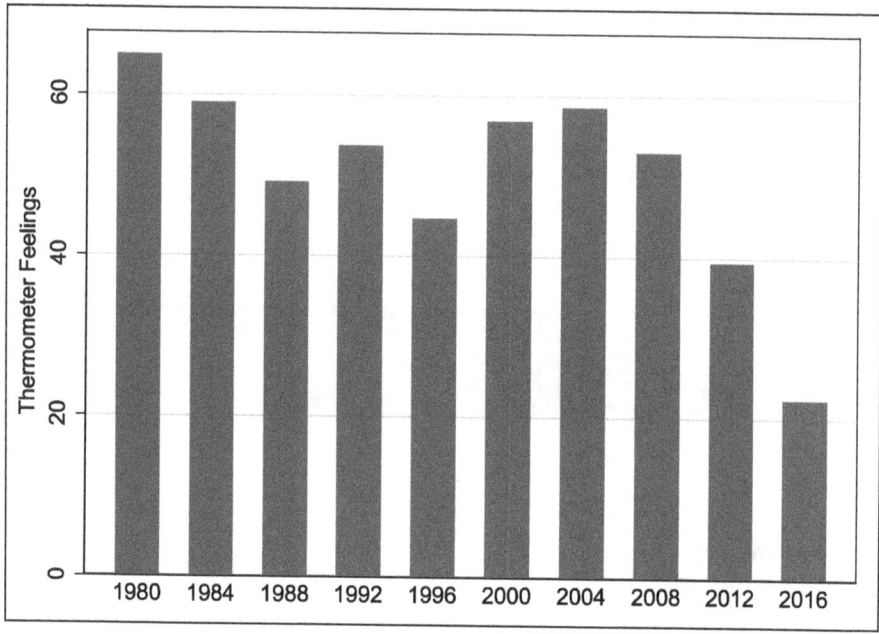

Fig. 26. Second-generation Mexican Americans' opinions of the Republican nominee from 1980 to 2016.

strongly suggests that Mexican Americans are disproportionately opposed to Trump's idea to build the wall.

The results in this section show that the theory is supported. There were differential differences as predicted, with second-generation Cuban Americans being more supportive of Trump and the Republican Party, with second-generation Mexican Americans being more opposed. These results confirm the importance of disaggregating the analysis of second-generation Americans by parental home country. Now, I examine second-generation Asian Americans.

Attitudes of Second-Generation Asian Americans, by Parental Home Country

The 2016 NAAS Post-Election study examines attitudes of representative samples of Americans with Bangladeshi, Cambodian, Chinese, Filipino, Hmong, Indian, Japanese, Korean, Pakistani, and Vietnamese ancestry. This survey is an essential resource because Asian Americans only make

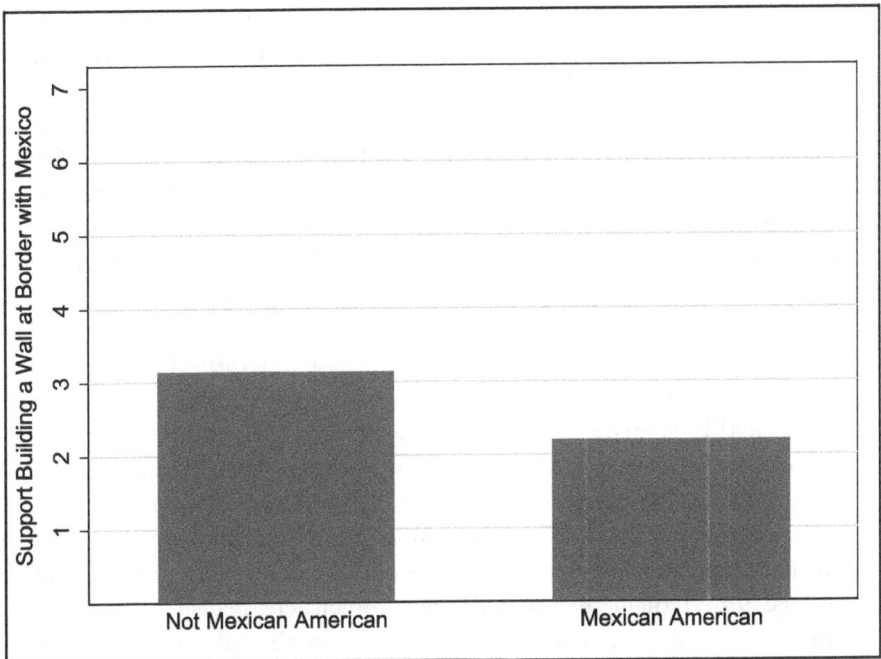

Fig. 27. Second-generation Mexican Americans' opinions on building the wall at Mexico's border in 2016.

up around 4% of the American population, and a random sample of the general population typically only includes a small number of Asian Americans. Subdividing that number by ancestry would therefore yield extremely small subsamples. To analyze differences between, for example, Vietnamese Americans and Japanese Americans requires a targeted sample of these populations. There need to be enough respondents so that the differences in the answers to the survey questions are discernible from random chance. The larger the sample drawn from a random population, the more the results can be attributable to actual attitudes and not random variations in a survey response. For example, the 2016 ANES survey only had 246 Asian Americans. Asian Americans represent the fastest-growing immigrant population, and it is vital to understand the differences between subpopulations in response to anti-immigration rhetoric and how they view the American party system.

Trump's relationship with the second-generation Asian American population is complicated by his general performance in office and how it may affect them, his policy toward parental birth countries in Asia (e.g., how his dealings with China may affect Chinese Americans directly), his policy towards immigration generally, and his intense anti-immigration rhetoric. While chapters 4 and 5 did not find differential responses for Asian Americans broadly to Trump's rhetoric, individual subgroups within the broader Asian American population may still have a negative attitude toward Trump. Using data from this survey, I will untangle the differential responses to the Trump presidency from second-generation Americans by parental home country subgroup.

As predicted, figure 28 shows that Vietnamese Americans had the most favorable impression of Trump after the 2016 election, while Bangladeshi Americans liked him the least. There was a statistically significant difference between Vietnamese Americans and the other Asian American subpopulations, with a pairwise correlation showing the difference is significant with a p-value of less than .01. Vietnamese Americans demonstrated their traditional partisan attachment to the Republican Party's nominee in 2016. The average for Vietnamese Americans was somewhere between somewhat unfavorable and somewhat favorable, and they are the only group to be on average favorable toward Trump. It is notable that, although their impression was the highest among second-generation Asian Americans, it was still not very favorable.

Notice as before with Latinos; there was no statistically significant difference between many of the other subgroups. For example, correlation analysis shows that the 95% confidence intervals overlapped for Japanese Americans and Korean Americans. On average, these groups had between a very unfavorable and a somewhat unfavorable impression of Trump.

An interesting pattern emerged from the data was a distinction between South Asian and East Asian respondents, with East Asian respondents having a slightly more favorable impression of Trump. As subsequent figures show, this pattern was persistent, so it is interesting to examine the differences between East Asians and South Asians in their development of partisan attachment in the United States. Significantly, this distinction was not driven by Vietnamese Americans alone because the average rating of Chinese and Cambodian Americans was significantly higher than that of Pakistani, Indian, or Bangladeshi Americans.

Turning to voting in 2016 by second-generation Americans subdivided by their parental home country, figure 29 shows that a large portion did not vote for Trump. The percentages are very low for many subgroups because

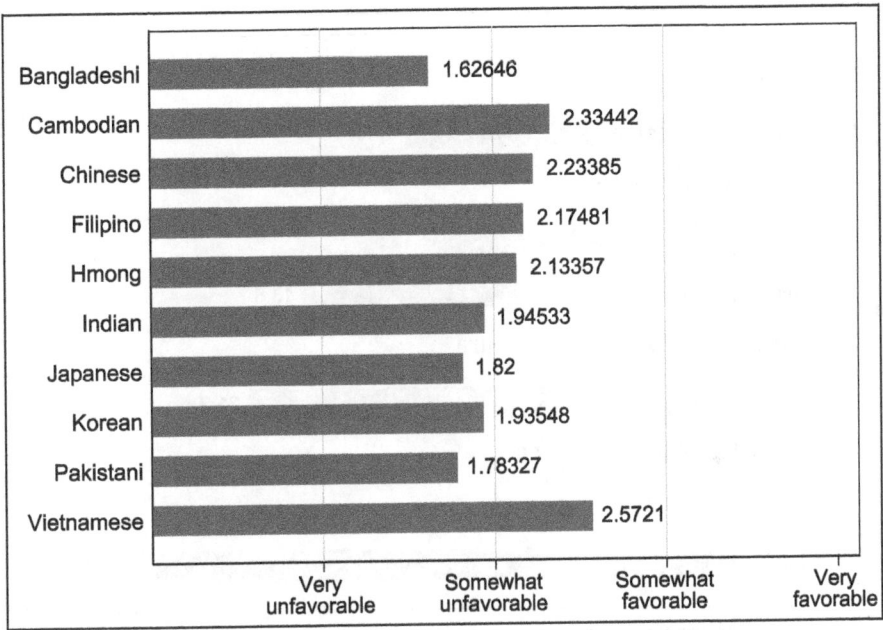

Fig. 28. Second-generation Asian Americans' impression of Trump in 2016, separated by parental home country.

second-generation Americans, in general, did not vote heavily for Trump. Further, Asian Americans were one of the racial groups that were least supportive of Trump in 2016, and the combination of being second generation and Asian American essentially equated to few votes for Trump in 2016.

Figure 29 also shows that Asian Americans from South Asia are less likely to vote for Trump in 2016. One subgroup that is slightly distinctive in this graph is the Chinese Americans, who voted for him at the second-lowest level. In comparison, only 3% of Pakistani Americans in the sample voted for him, which is an extremely low number. To put this in perspective, Trump won 11% of the black vote in 2016 and anywhere between 22% and 30% of the Latino vote. Thus, we observe again the distinction that second-generation Americans with South Asian ancestry were more likely to be resistant to Trump than East Asian Americans in this sample.

For example, figure 29 shows that slightly more than 21% of second-generation Japanese Americans reported voting for Trump in the 2016 election. That is a significant level of support for a candidate who, some estimates show, received votes from only about 15% of all second-

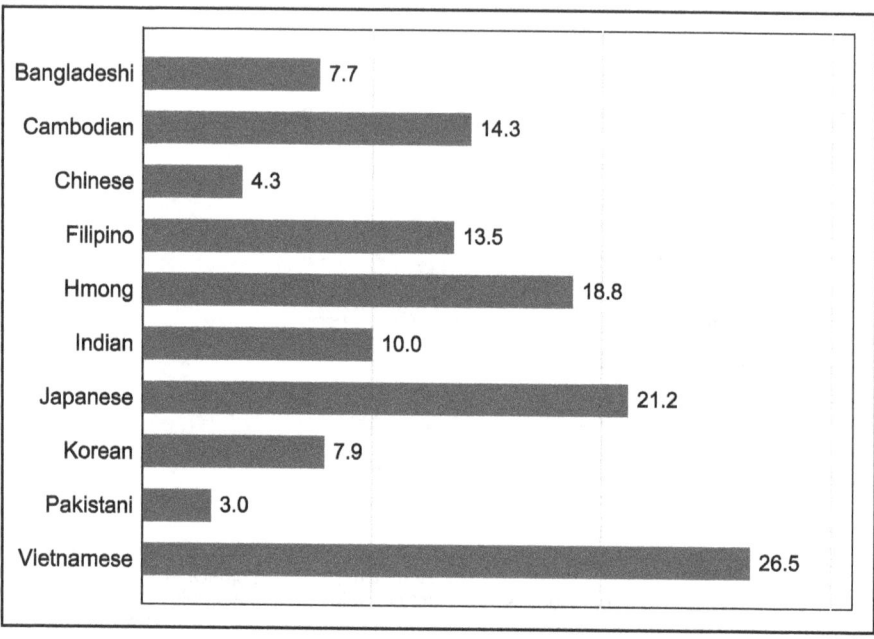

Fig. 29. Percentage of second-generation Asian Americans voting for Trump in 2016, separated by parental home country.

generation Americans in the 2016 election. This finding shows the importance of empirically analyzing these subgroups because their vote choices are not predetermined by race or immigrant generation. These Americans have diverse beliefs. Some of them would be politically conservative and would have chosen Trump because he was the candidate that best matched their political views. Conversely, the data also showed that 80% of Japanese Americans did not vote for Trump.

Figure 30 shows party identification of the second-generation Asian Americans divided by parental home country. Vietnamese Americans are still more strongly associated with the Republican Party than most other second-generation Asian Americans; however, the figure shows that the diversity in party identification may not be fully appreciated. For example, second-generation Korean Americans have the largest identification with the Republican Party at 35%, while Hmong Americans are the lowest at 14%. Importantly, no group of second-generation Americans is even close to 50%. This suggests going forward that the impact of the Trump administration may last far beyond his one-term presidency because party identification tends to last a long time.

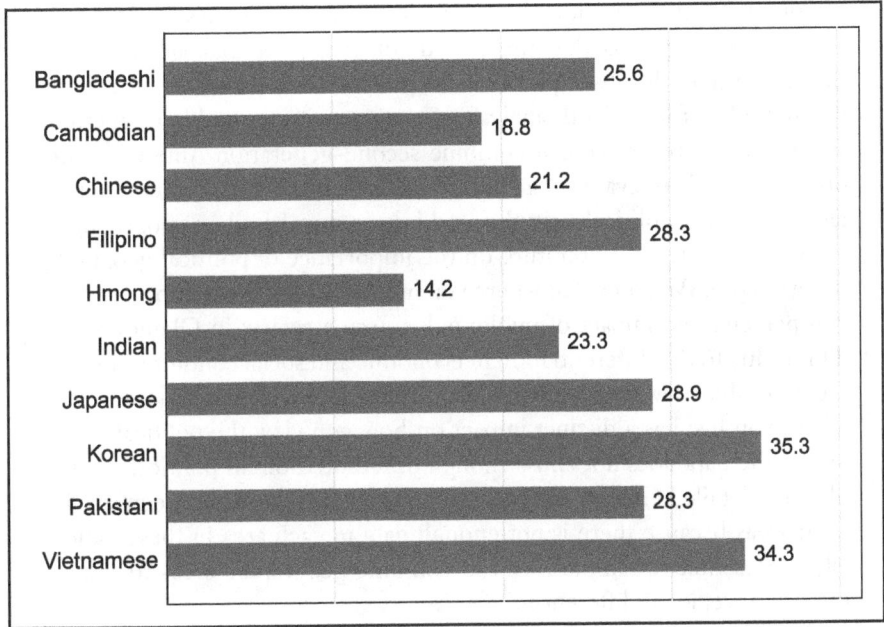

Fig. 30. Percentage of second-generation Asian Americans identifying with the Republican Party in 2016, separated by parental home country.

As with Latino Americans, the theory was generally supported when analyzing second-generation Asian Americans' attitudes toward Trump and the Republican Party by parental home country. As predicted, Vietnamese Americans were the most supportive of Trump and the Republican Party in this time. Also, note that a consistent distinction between East Asian and South Asian second-generation Americans was uncovered. This again verifies the importance of not generalizing across subethnic groups and analyzing important subgroups within second-generation Americans. I now examine another way that second-generation Americans' attitudes toward Trump's rhetoric can be disaggregated, political geography.

Political Geography and Attitudes of Second-Generation Americans

While ancestry is an interesting way to differentiate second-generation Americans, it is not the only way. The data does not allow a deep dive into the disproportionate impact on categories within each ancestral group because there is not enough data, such as the difference between male and female

Hmong second-generation Americans. Even in the samples that targeted these ancestral groups, the samples did not have more than around 300 at the largest in each subsample. This creates statistical power problems that will not allow for in-depth analysis of many categories within each ethnic subgroup. However, we can combine second-generation Americans into other politically relevant subgroups to examine the effect of other potential factors on their political attitudes, and I do so now based on geography.

There is extensive literature on the importance of political geography (Short 1993). We know that where you live has a significant impact on how you perceive the impact of public policy (see a review in Okunev 2021). This is due to the differentiation in economic and social conditions in lived areas combined with political culture differences. It is well known that where you live has a distinct impact on how you view the political world. While the data does not allow enough differentiation on political geography at a detailed enough level to examine the differences between specific local areas because there is not enough data in each area in these nationally representative samples, we can combine geographic areas to analyze important regional differences.

For Trump in 2016, the most important regional difference was the border states with Mexico due to his intense rhetoric over building the wall there to stop illegal immigration. We can expect those second-generation Americans that live in these areas to be disproportionately impacted by building a wall with Mexico. As such, it is interesting to examine the differential impact on second-generation Americans who live near the border to those who do not live near it on attitudes toward Trump's idea of building the wall.

Figure 31 shows answers to the same question that was asked about Trump's idea of building the wall with Mexico in 2016 used in figure 27. In this bar graph, second-generation Americans are broken down into those who live in border states and those who do not. The border states are Texas, New Mexico, Arizona, and California. We see a statistically significant difference in opposition to building the wall for second-generation Americans who live in border states. The mean level of opposition for those living in a border state was 5.33, and for those not living in a border state, it was 4.92, on a scale of 1 to 7, with 7 equaling the greatest opposition. A pairwise correlation between opposition to building the wall and living in a border state shows a .087 coefficient with a p-value of .042. Ordered logistic regression models also show a statistically significant negative impact from living in border states for second-generation Americans' opinion

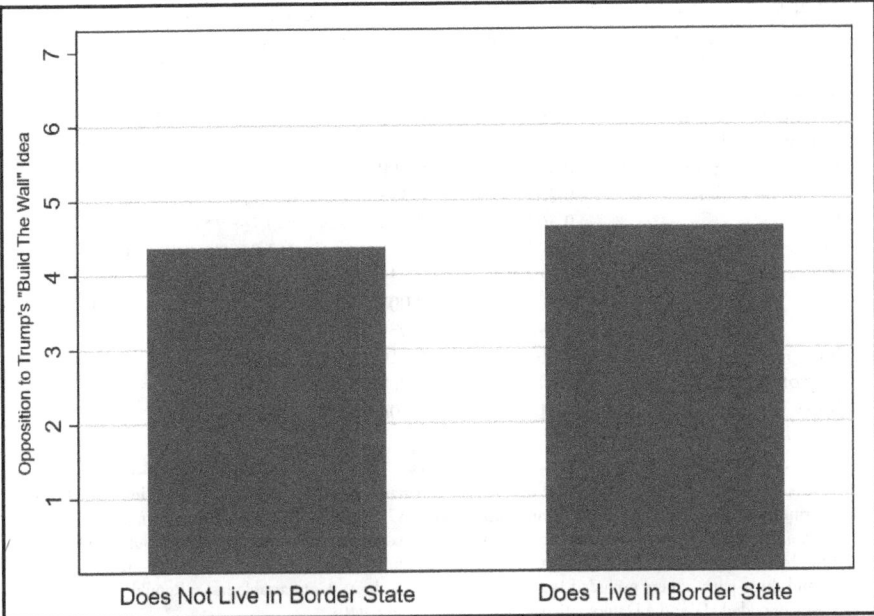

Fig. 31. Second-generation Americans' opinions on building the wall at Mexico's border in 2016 by border state residency.

about Trump's idea to build the wall with Mexico. The odds ratio of opposition to building the wall for those second-generation Americans living in border states is 1.48 with a p-value of 0.018.

These results clearly show that another way to disaggregate second-generation Americans' attitudes after exposure to Trump's rhetoric is by political geography. Although the data available does not allow an in-depth analysis of community-by-community differentiation, it is highly plausible that such differentiation does exist and is vital to understanding attitudes of second-generation Americans more broadly. I leave it to future researchers to delve deeper into the importance of political geography and incorporation in America.

The Influence of Party Identification on Second-Generation American Voting

Another way that second generation Americans are differentiated is by their partisan identification. While the theory presupposes that many will not have strong predispositions toward the party system, some will, and it

TABLE 18. Determinants of Voting for a Republican Presidential Candidate for Second-Generation American Democrats and Republicans, 1952 to 2020

Variable	Democrats	S.E.	Republicans	S.E.
Second generation × Trump on ballot	0.161	0.542	−0.506*	0.226
Second generation	−0.314	0.190	−0.152	0.177
Trump on ballot	0.261	0.335	0.170	0.259
Hispanic	−0.509**	0.195	−0.768***	0.113
Black	−2.022***	0.291	−2.747***	0.337
Education	−0.119**	0.043	0.037	0.077
Age	−0.001	0.003	0.012***	0.002
Male	−0.092	0.089	0.205	0.143
Income	−0.063***	0.016	−0.028***	0.007
Year of election	−0.044***	0.008	−0.003	0.010
Intercept	86.812***	16.206	8.336	20.472
N	10,213		8,063	

Note: Cells represent unstandardized coefficients and standard errors for logistic regression models for determinants of voting for a Republican presidential candidate from 1952 in 2020. The models are for being either second-generation American Democrats or second-generation American Republicans, measured by self-expressed party identification. The dependent variable is two-party vote share, with nonvoters and third-party voters excluded from the analysis. The dependent variable has a Republican vote for president coded (1), and a Democratic vote for president coded (0).

+$p < .10$, *$p < .05$, **$p < .01$, ***$p < .001$

is interesting to examine the impact of partisan identification on voting for Trump. To examine those second-generation immigrants that self-identify as Republican versus those that self-identify as Democrat, table 18 shows unstandardized coefficients and standard errors for logistic regression models for determinants of voting for a Republican presidential candidate from 1952 to 2020. The models are for being either second-generation American Democrats or Republicans, measured by self-expressed party identification. The dependent variable is two-party vote share, with nonvoters and third-party voters excluded from the analysis. The dependent variable has a Republican vote for President coded (1), and a Democratic vote for President coded (0).

The results show that second-generation American Republicans are less likely than non-second-generation Republicans to vote for Trump across all model specifications. This finding replicates the work in chapter 6, which showed that the treatment effect is larger for conservative second-generation Americans. Democratic second-generation Americans are not statistically significantly different than non-second-generation Democrats in the rate of voting for Trump from non-second-generation Americans.

The lack of statistical significance for Democratic second-generation Americans is probably due to the very low level of Republican voting from second-generation American Democrats even before Trump.

Conclusion

The chapter has clearly shown that there are some distinctions based on subethnic groupings. As originally hypothesized, Vietnamese Americans and Cuban Americans are more likely to view the Republican Party and Donald Trump positively than other members of their pan-ethnic groups. For the other subgroups, across almost every category, there is little difference between most subgroupings regarding their attitudes toward the Republican Party or Trump's impact. There are no statistically significant differences across several measures analyzed in this chapter from the other subgroups. Unlike the previous chapter, this outcome is not explainable by statistical power issues because these surveys have hundreds of members of these subgroups. The two groups that feature profoundly stark differences from the other subgroups are Vietnamese Americans and Cuban Americans. Thus, this chapter's chief finding is that second-generation Americans do not differ significantly by parental home country in their attitudes toward Donald Trump or the Republican Party, except Vietnamese Americans and Cuban Americans are more positive, and Mexican Americans are more negative. Second-generation Americans living in border states were also found to be more resistant to Trump's ideas, such as the idea of building a wall between Mexico and the United States. I also found that Republican second-generation Americans are less likely to vote for Trump than other Republicans, even though they are still more likely to vote for Trump than non-Republican second-generation Americans.

The most straightforward explanation for the finding regarding Vietnamese Americans and Cuban Americans is their long-standing identification with the Republican Party. Through motivated reasoning, partisan identification creates a positive view of their party's actions (see Nir 2011). Motivated reasoning implies that people will search for interpretations and explanations for behavior that they find cognitively dissonant (Lodge and Taber 2013). Cognitive dissonance is the process by which new information comes into conflict with prior beliefs. Reagan, in particular, established with these groups that the Republican Party was on their side because of his clear anticommunism and tough stances with the Castro regime and the Communist Party of Vietnam. These Republican-leaning subgroups may disproportionately view negative information about the Republican Party and its presidential nominee as dissonant to what they previously believed. Furthermore, experimental research has shown that the impact of prior beliefs on subsequent beliefs and behavior is profound (e.g., Westen et al. 2006). As such, it is not surprising that these groups—which are the only subethnic groups that have a long-standing relationship with the Republican Party—viewed the Republican presidential nominee more favorably than other groups even though his rhetoric bashed immigrants similar to their own families.

As the second-generation ages and is replaced by third- and fourth-generation Vietnamese Americans and Cuban Americans, the opposition to these regimes and communism may no longer carry as much weight. The Castro era has ended in Cuba, and Vietnamese communism is deeply intertwined with American capitalism through outsourcing and globalization. Moreover, while both nations are repressive—Freedom House classifies both nations are not free—they are not as brutal as the regimes that drove the second-generation's parents away. If Cuba and Vietnam democratize, or at least become less repressive, the third- and fourth-generation Vietnamese Americans and Cuban Americans may reassess the Republican Party based more on current domestic politics than on past history. If the Republican Party continues to alienate Asian Americans and Latinos, third- and fourth-generation Vietnamese Americans and Cuban Americans may be less inclined to support Republicans to the same extent as earlier generations.

Another interesting finding is the relatively lower support for the Republican Party and more negative views of Trump among South Asians than among East Asians. The data show that Bangladeshi, Pakistani, and Indian Americans were more likely to have negative feelings toward the Republican Party and view Donald Trump's actions as more detrimental. The differences are not always statistically significant, but the pattern is clear across almost every measurement in this chapter. Thoroughly understanding South Asian Americans' relationship toward conservativism and the Republican Party seems to be a potentially significant development for the future of American politics because Indian Americans are the largest immigrant group entering America in 2021.

I now conclude this book's findings in the final chapter and offer seven potential ways that this book could suggest paths for future scholarship.

References

Eckstein, Susan. 2009. *The Immigrant Divide: How Cuban Americans Changed the US and Their Homeland.* New York: Routledge Press.

Garcia, Maria Cristina. 1996. *Havana USA: Cuban Exiles and Cuban Americans in South Florida, 1959–1994.* Berkeley: University of California Press.

Hajnal, Zoltan L., and Taeku Lee. 2011. *Why Americans Don't Join the Party: Race, Immigration, and the Failure (of Political Parties) to Engage the Electorate.* Princeton: Princeton University Press.

Le, Loan Kieu, and Phi Hong Su. 2018. "Party Identification and the Immigrant Cohort Hypothesis: The Case of Vietnamese Americans." *Politics, Groups, and Identities* 6 (4): 743–63.

Lodge, Milton, and Charles Taber. 2013. *The Rationalizing Voter.* New York: Cambridge University Press.

Nir, Lilach. 2011. "Motivated Reasoning and Public Opinion Perception." *Public Opinion Quarterly* 75 (3): 504–32.

Okunev, Igor. 2021. *Political Geography.* Brussels: Peter Lang Press.

Ramakrishnan, Karthick, Jennifer Lee, Taeku Lee, and Janelle Wong. 2018. "National Asian American Survey (NAAS) 2016 Post-Election Survey." Riverside, CA: National Asian American Survey.

Short, J. R. 1993. *An Introduction to Political Geography.* London: Routledge Press.

Westen, D., P. S. Blagov, K. Harenski, C. Kilts, and S. Hamann. 2006. "Neural Bases of Motivated Reasoning: An fMRI Study of Emotional Constraints on Partisan Political Judgment in the 2004 US Presidential Election." *Journal of Cognitive Neuroscience* 18 (11): 1947–58.

Zhou, Min, and Yang Sao Xiong. 2005. "The Multifaceted American Experiences of the Children of Asian Immigrants: Lessons for Segmented Assimilation." *Ethnic and Racial Studies* 28 (6): 1119–52.

CHAPTER 8

Conclusion

This book shows the importance of understanding the impact of political communication on immigrant incorporation. My collateral damage theory describes how anti-immigrant elite rhetoric lessens the attraction for incorporating into the United States and reduces support for the Republican Party. I also theorize that not all immigrants fit my thesis, specifically Cuban Americans, Vietnamese Americans, and Mexican Americas. I tested these ideas with a series of experiments using online samples matched to nationally representative census data for second-generation Americans, which were buttressed by decades of aggregate and newly collected survey data. This chapter provides a brief overview of the findings, speculates on the future of immigrant incorporation, and highlights seven critical areas where research is still needed.

Using a theoretical approach from social psychology adapted from communication science, I stated four lemmas necessary for my theory to be valid. I showed that each of these necessary conditions is currently present in the United States: (1) the rhetoric has been broadcast widely enough that most second-generation Americans will have been exposed to it; (2) second-generation Americans are deeply interested in immigration; (3) they also have less political socialization into American political institutions; and, finally, (4) I showed no rational or expressed desire for these consequences from Donald Trump. With these four lemmas established, I then showed in-depth how the rhetoric of Trump is strongly anti-immigrant. Although this conclusion may be intuitive to anyone who follows American politics, it has previously not been empirically shown.

Based on the theory and the subsequent proof that the conditions necessary for rhetoric to be influential were present, I conducted experiments using nationally representative samples and showed that the theoretically predicted outcomes were manifested. My findings show that exposure to Trump's anti-immigration rhetoric reduced the likelihood of expressed patriotism, American identity, and support for the Republican Party. These findings have profound implications for American politics in the coming decades due to the large population of second-generation Americans. Further, while their parents were not Americans and may not have transmitted an intense political socialization process to their children, second-generation Americans grew up in the United States and more than likely will pass on these anti-Republican beliefs to their children and their grandchildren. Thus, Trump's rhetoric can plausibly have an intergenerational impact that negatively affects the Republican Party for many years.

In sum, my theory of collateral damage was shown to be correct. Trump's rhetoric has lessened the desire for incorporation into the United States and the Republican Party. As such, it is essential to consider how incorporation may proceed in the future for the children of immigrants in the post-Trump United States.

The Future of Immigrant Incorporation

The level of support for incorporating second-generation Americans in the United States is typically ascertained using survey data. Survey research examines who supports incorporation, views themselves as incorporated, and values retaining a distinct cultural identity and not incorporating it into the larger American society. The results show that many of the fears that second-generation Americans will not want to incorporate are unfounded because large numbers of them typically view incorporation as generally beneficial. They also view more specific factors, such as speaking English, getting an education, joining the military, and buying a home, in a positive light. Further, intermarriage between second-generation Americans and non-second-generation Americans is common, and survey data indicate that it is viewed as nonproblematic, traditionally a measurement of the assimilation process. None of the research suggests that the current wave of immigrants and their children will not follow the traditional process of step-by-step incorporation in which each generation becomes increasingly more a part of the American system.

Research has also examined which factors impact supporting incorporation, and the results show that traditional explanations have explanatory power. Specifically, ethnicity, religiosity, ideology, partisan identification, education, income, gender, and parents' length of time in the United States significantly impact support or opposition to incorporation. Interestingly, political interest and media consumption increase exposure to anti-immigrant rhetoric from politicians and are also strongly significant negative predictors of incorporation, suggesting that the current political environment influences attitudes toward incorporation.

In addition, while the empirical evidence does not support deep fears and concerns, it does highlight diverse levels of incorporation and beliefs about the United States among second-generation Americans. The civic engagement of the children of immigrants was often as high or higher than other Americans, but a greater proportion of them expressed that they dislike everyday life in the United States. Feelings of American identity were rated similarly on average but had a bimodal distribution for individuals with two foreign-born parents than those with two native-born parents. The data on educational attainment, employment, homeownership, and military service showed diverse outcomes and general heterogeneity for various factors, including gender, race, and parents' home country. Similar results found support for political parties, voter turnout, and other forms of political participation and party contact. In sum, various measures of immigrant incorporation showed a diverse group that is both similar and dissimilar to other Americans in levels of societal and political engagement.

Thus, one possibility is that the future of incorporation may be like the past, where the current wave of immigrants and their descendants become fully incorporated into the American political system. Although Trump's rhetoric appears to be damaging to the Republican Party and may in some ways undermine peoples' attitudes toward the United States, he was only a one-term president. If subsequent politicians use less harsh rhetoric, then the impact from Trump will be diminished. If, however, the Republican Party continues to indulge in immigrant-bashing in the future, then we can expect a potentially different incorporation process that has happened in the past.

Based on these divergent potential outcomes, I now suggest seven topics related to this book's findings that need more in-depth research.

Seven Topics Needing More Research

These results naturally lead to insights on other research topics. The following seven topics could be influenced by communicative processes similar to those that undergird my theoretical model. These topics are on critical political processes that can be influenced by rhetoric or affect immigrant incorporation. I start by examining one of Trump's rhetoric's most discussed aspects, namely, his influence on his supporters' beliefs and behaviors.

Trump's Impact on Supporters

Does hateful speech by politicians get amplified by their supporters? Trump has not openly advocated for violently attacking immigrants, but many people have held him responsible for his followers' violent attacks. Can Trump's rhetoric be blamed if his followers go beyond what he is advocating? During the attack on the US Capitol in January 2021, most commentators blamed Trump's intense rhetoric for inciting the violent mob. This accusation was the basis of his second impeachment trial. Similarly, during the United States' long history, intense protests, riots, and other criminal activities against immigrants have commonly been blamed on politicians' hateful remarks. However, these criminal actions often far exceed what these politicians advocated. We do not know if elite hate speech leads to even greater violence than was advocated for, and the minimal effects paradigm would cast doubt on this assertion.

We know that politicians may influence the views of those that listen to them, with predictable mediated effects based on political and sociological homophily. Some politicians routinely make hateful comments about marginalized groups, often a racial or ethnic minority, but also about others. The theoretical and empirical insights from the framing literature are vast. The standard framing theory suggests that supporters would be influenced in a probabilistic way to increase their feeling toward the group in the direction of the hate speech, that is, to be more opposed to the disparaged out-group. However, this hypothesis has another version.

This commonly spoken-of but not empirically tested hypothesis posits that listeners will become hateful beyond what is suggested by the politician's original disparaging remarks. Two different reasons may explain this outcome. First, social desirability may initially hinder these listeners' hateful actions. Once they receive a signal from an elite source that it is socially acceptable to attack the group, they will do so at their actual level of hatred, which may be well beyond the elite's expressed level of animosity. I term this *revealing* because it reveals the actual level of hate, even though it appears as though hearing the politician's hateful remarks amplified their animosity.

The second path is what I term *amplification*. Here, if a societal elite starts to trash-and-bash a particular group, individuals within the receptive public will increase existing hatred toward that group. Once the politician triggers the increase, the hatred spirals upward and out of control, leading to ever greater fury against the group. Opponents often scold politicians that their words will lead to "even greater" assaults against the out-group, but whether the assaults are even greater or merely the same has not been tested empirically. For example, recent attacks on Asian Americans related to the COVID-19 pandemic go far beyond Trump's rhetoric of "Chinese virus" and "kung flu" in attributing blame for COVID-19 to the Chinese.

These pathways are different from simple framing because they lead to greater hateful actions than the politician initially suggested. Moving past the original point of the politician's message, a different subset of framing emerges compared with what traditional studies have examined, which merely suggests an influence of—or at most convergence with—the speaker. Future researchers can use this book's insights to develop theoretical models of anti-immigration rhetoric's influence on political violence.

The Impact of Anti-Incorporation Pressure

Another topic for future researchers is the impact of anti-incorporation pressure. The unpacked assumption of many ethnic studies is that immigrants desire to remain culturally distinct.[1] Brubaker (2001) calls this assumption the "differentialist turn" and notes that immigrants' supposed opposition to incorporation has been the dominant paradigm in political science, sociology, and related fields since the 1970s (see also Appiah 2005 for a cogent explanation of these assumptions and their problems). This paradigm suggests that immigrants do not actually want to incorporate but are simply pressured to do so.

Problematically, researchers' assumptions that the descendants of recent immigrants resist America's pro-incorporation culture may have led them to ignore what I term *anti-incorporation pressures*. Although some scholars have examined the pressures that minorities within the same group place on each other not to incorporate, almost no one studies the pressure applied by majority members on minorities not to incorporate. This phenomenon needs to be examined. It is crucial to determine whether the

---

1. See Hollinger (2006) for a review of the intellectual history of incorporation and multiculturalism.

dominant research paradigm—the differentialist turn—is correct because many second-generation Americans' behavior does not match the theory's assumptions.

Anti-incorporation pressure may occur when majority-culture members put social pressure on minorities to remain culturally distinct. The discrimination faced by immigrants and their children may be greater than currently acknowledged because scholars ignore anti-incorporation pressure. Scholars may ignore discrimination arising from an overfocus on a person's differences rather than their cultural similarities. We can only know whether immigrants feel pressured to stay culturally distinct by asking them, but scant academic research has investigated this question as yet. Consequently, the dominant research paradigm is not complete or even empirically correct. Many second-generation Americans support incorporation, and we should expect them to incorporate *if they are unencumbered by social pressure not to incorporate*.

Many second-generation Americans view themselves as typical Americans, and suggestions to the contrary are perceived as insulting, suggesting that they value incorporation. Scholars have assumed Americans want incorporation from immigrants without empirically analyzing other perspectives. Researchers should investigate whether second-generation Americans are offended by pressure to incorporate and pressure to remain culturally distinct.

Microaggressions and Lack of Intention

Similarly, the microaggression literature documents how small slights and insults accumulate over the years and take a sizeable psychological toll (Wing Sue et al. 2007). The idea of microaggressions has only been commonly discussed since Wing Sue et al. (2007). Microaggressions can be defined as seemingly insignificant comments or actions that subtly insult, condescend to, humiliate, or degrade a person who is a member of a minority group. A vital part of this definition is the word "minority" because it is assumed that a person from the majority group will have enough social power not to be damaged by such comments. These comments are far from insignificant for a person affected by them, creating lasting harm.

Everyday snide or uncaring remarks often seem trivial in isolation, but in combination they can be hurtful (Campbell and Manning 2014). Due to the personal remarks appearing to be trivial, past researchers often ignored their overall impact. Commonplace discourse from members of various minority groups reveals the omnipresence of condescending insults (McCabe 2009). Frustration is increased because the person who has been insulted either seems hostile for taking umbrage at a trivial remark or feels compelled to leave it unchallenged to avoid seeming hostile.

Often, these comments accentuate a person's differences, such as asking an Asian American, "What's your nationality?"[2] when there is no reason to assume that they were born outside the United States. Another example is telling a Hispanic American, "You speak good English." This comment emphasizes and aggrandizes differences to the point of becoming exclusionary because it demonstrates the assumption that the Hispanic American's native language is not English (or that they were probably not born in the United States).

Just as this book shows that hostile elite rhetoric inhibits incorporation, everyday political discussions that feature microaggressions may also inhibit incorporation. This is a potential area where future researchers can use the theoretical model developed in the book in subsequent research on the nexus of communication and incorporation.

Are Refugees Similarly Affected by Trump's Rhetoric?

Trump has often bashed refugees, and these populations may have experienced an effect similar to that experienced by immigrants. The resettlement of displaced peoples is profoundly important, and it is crucial to know whether and how the government's effectiveness in responding to resettlement influences the civic engagement and political participation of displaced peoples. The benefits of civic engagement have been shown in many settings, with societies with more civic engagement being more efficient and better working, as shown by the greater presence of normatively desirable properties such as equality and health (Putnam 2000). Successfully integrating displaced people into a country's social and political fabric is crucial for modern advanced industrial democracies. We do not know enough about how such populations will integrate into their host societies if prominent anti-refugee elite rhetoric is present. My findings strongly suggest that anti-refugee rhetoric will harm refugees' willingness to incorporate into the host society. Future researchers should investigate this topic in greater depth.

---

2. The microaggression examples in this paragraph are taken from Wing Sue et al. (2007).

Impact on Social Trust

Another topic needing further investigation is the impact of heated rhetoric on social trust. Interest in this topic has recently surged. Trust and cooperation form the basis for almost all human success. The most intractable social problems are essentially collective action problems, from stopping global warming to ending civil wars and resolving pandemics. However, solving these problems is inherently difficult due to differing incentives for individuals within groups and each group as a whole.

For example, it may be beneficial for a member to cheat others in their group, even though it is detrimental to their entire well-being. More perversely, as all members know that this cheating is possible, some may cheat the group to avoid being taken advantage of by others. This logic commonly leads to suboptimal performance of the group and possibly to its eventual destruction. Hence, overcoming cheating and shirking is central to any cooperative endeavor. If elites' intense, belligerent rhetoric decreases willingness to trust and cooperate with marginalized groups, it could have a profoundly negative impact on the willingness to engage in collective action problem solving through mutual sacrifice. Future researchers should study the impact of belligerent harsh rhetoric on social cohesion and social trust.

Reforms Designed to Increase Incorporation

Another interesting and understudied topic is whether everyday institutions can be changed to encourage immigrants to incorporate into the broader American society. This open question is crucial because comprehensive immigration reform will permanently add millions of immigrants to the United States if passed. This book shows that part of the answer depends upon how the country treats immigrants, which will affect how they view the desirability of incorporation. A large body of literature indicates that civic education is crucial for citizenship training (Camicia and Saavedra 2009), while service-learning and training programs promote political participation (Furco and Root 2010).

However, researchers stress that a focus on immigrants' perceptions and problems is necessary for incorporation to be successful (Downs 2012). Spencer (2011) found that overly flowery depictions of the United States are unconvincing to people whose real-life problems create an entirely different picture. Identity is crucial to understanding who chooses to become civically engaged and patriotic (Osanloo 2011). Deaux (2011) found this to be particularly true for immigrants, who have to navigate diverse meanings associated with American identity. An institutional reform that takes identities seriously by treating complaints as legitimate will be more likely to engage them. One approach is to openly admit that the United States has problems while simultaneously showing that it cares enough about its people to fix those problems.

The constant praise of the United States that is typical of some civic education may turn off immigrants who are well aware of the country's problems. However, focusing exclusively on these problems will not inspire trust or confidence or build efficacy because it will not show the United States' positive side. Perhaps the key is to create programs that allow input on problems and lead to real success in fixing them. Behavioral economics studies show that small trust-building exercises lead to greater cooperation. Such exercises openly admit that problems exist, but they also show how to work within the system to solve them.

Critics of civic education often complain that it is a type of propaganda that leads to nationalistic patriotism (for a review of these criticisms, see Nussbaum 2012). They suggest that citizens remain critical of the system rather than be forced into programs that reinforce nationalistic patriotism (Pompa 2002). Some authors in political philosophy suggest that efforts to promote patriotism are detrimental because citizens will lose their ability to critique society (MacIntyre 1995; Kateb 2006).

Successful reform efforts would teach immigrant children the two principles of constructive patriotism: specifically, the United States has problems and that its people can work together to fix those problems. Critical patriotism could be used as a method to inspire joint sacrifice and commitment. The lesson is that problems occur in a democratic society, but you can fix them if you work within the system. This approach can reach skeptical individuals turned off by talking about the United States in too positive a way. This approach indicates that recognizing America's problems is patriotic as long as you work within the system to solve them. It rejects both nihilistic anti-Americanism and belligerent nationalistic patriotism and can profoundly influence a successful new civic education. What is lacking is research on instilling constructive patriotism and its down-the-line effects on civic engagement and political participation.

Impact of Anti-Immigration Rhetoric Outside the United States

Also of interest is that many countries have seen an explosion of anti-immigration rhetoric since the advent of globalization. An essential expansion of the research in this book would be to examine whether its findings hold outside the political and cultural context of the United States. An extensive literature exists on cross-cultural social psychology (see Shiraev and Levy 2007 and Smith, Bond, and Kâgitçibasi 2006 for recent reviews), and these studies show that the treatment effects of experimental stimuli differ across cultural contexts (Adler and Gielen 2001). The methodology uses multinational research sites to leverage cultural variables that are intractable when using within-country designs (Brislin 2000). It is nearly impossible to test the political impact of culture on citizens from the same nation because they often do not differ much concerning cultural variables. To test the effect of culture, it is beneficial to compare the experimental results from one culture to another (Chryssochoou 2003). A common intuitive approach is to conduct an identical experiment using participants from multiple nations (Goldstein 2000). This approach allows the researcher to examine the treatment effect under various cultural constraints.

Sometimes, these culturally dependent treatment effects are strongly counterintuitive and provide great insight. A compelling example is a study by Yamagishi and Yamagishi (1994), who showed that Japanese participants are more likely than American participants to cheat in a prisoner's dilemma game on a computer. The authors conducted this experiment within a more extensive study on how the meaning of trust varies by cultural context. The theory of assurance derived from this cross-cultural study is now commonly used, for example, in studies on social capital (Yamagishi 2003). This is an often-cited classic study that would not have been possible without the cross-cultural design of the same experiment conducted in Japan and the United States.

Immigration inherently brings different peoples into a country, and how the host society receives newcomers is influenced by national legitimizing myths, which influence the acceptance of outsiders (Pratto and Lemieux 2001). Research shows that Japan's national myths emphasize essentialist difference and isolation (Dale 1986), and immigrants acting like Japanese people—that is, assimilating—may be repulsive to Japanese xenophobes. Prior research shows a link between attitudes against assimilation in Japan and a lack of support for immigration (Richey 2010). In contrast, research shows that Americans desire assimilation from immigrants because it matches their view of what US history and culture require (Bourhis et al. 1997). The various national myths make assimilation mean different things in different contexts. The American conception of xenophobia suggests that xenophobes will demand assimilation from immigrants, while

Japanese history shows that support for assimilation is common among non-xenophobes.

However, most scholars study America, and they, therefore, examine a heterogeneous culture that emphasizes assimilation (e.g., Hollinger 2006). This point is important because the underlying assumptions of assimilationism are related to the contact hypothesis. Assimilationism posits that it is beneficial for immigrants to join and work together with the host society thoroughly to be less divided and better functioning (e.g., Huntington 2004). This view of assimilationism is related to the contact hypothesis's central concept whereby groups working together will increase harmony. If a native-born person is resistant to assimilation, the increased contact with assimilated immigrants may increase dislike and provoke disharmony. Thus, the cultural impetus for whether immigrants should assimilate or not may influence the impact of intergroup contact. Future research should test whether the impact of anti-immigration rhetoric varies by cultural contexts with different values on assimilation.

I now discuss the limitations of this book.

Limitations of This Research

While the research in this book has clearly demonstrated that within the period that these survey samples were taken, there is a negative impact from anti-immigration rhetoric on incorporation for second-generation Americans within America broadly and the Republican Party more specifically. However, two chief limitations cannot be addressed with these types of data and research designs. First, it is highly plausible that local environments—and citizens' interaction within these environments—produce localized impacts and understandings of elite rhetoric. These processes can both be encouraged and discouraged by the interactions of the citizen within their social environment.

Most importantly for this research, these localized interactions can moderate and mediate the impact of the anti-immigration rhetoric. For example, it is highly likely that if someone lives in an area with intense wage competition due to immigration, they may perceive anti-immigration rhetoric from elites differently from those who are not living in environments with direct wage competition. The research designs used in this book cannot examine the interaction between the local environment and elite rhetoric in this book.

Further, there is extensive literature on the contact hypothesis, which states simply that if you have more contact with someone, you will see past stereotypes and simplified understandings of them based on their group and see the actual person's traits. The more you interact with someone from a different group, the research finds, the more likely you will have a positive interpretation based on these interactions. Localized environments that promote more in-depth contact between second-generation Americans and those outside the second generation may moderate the effect of elite rhetoric. Whether they have been treated positively or negatively by their neighbors will change how they interpret elite rhetoric based on whether the anti-immigration rhetoric agrees with the treatment by their neighbors. The research designs cannot address political geography in this book, and it is a limitation in our complete understanding of how elite rhetoric affects immigration processes.

Additionally, all of the empirical evidence that has been gathered in this book comes from the last 40 years, and the vast majority of it has been collected in the Trump era—roughly defined from 2015 until 2021. As shown in chapter 3, the Trump era is unique in that we have never had a presidential nominee or president who has spoken with such intense interest in or as negatively toward immigration as Trump. Because this book analyzes experiments and survey data taken primarily from the Trump era, it cannot make a comprehensive historical analysis of the effects of anti-immigrant rhetoric on incorporation. Other eras that featured anti-immigration rhetoric but at a different level with different social, technological, and economic environments may produce different effects than what was found in this book. The empirical strategies of this book are limited in that they do not allow a broad historical context.

However, the Trump era has been long enough that we can expect some long-term impact. Furthermore, as of this book's writing, Trump has expressed interest in remaining involved in American politics and sends daily missives to his gigantic email list blasting immigration among other topics. If his anti-immigration rhetoric continues for even another presidential election cycle, that will entail an entire decade of intense anti-immigration rhetoric at a level that we have not seen before. Thus, understanding the Trump era precisely without analyzing broader historical concepts is still essential because it has become an entire era of American politics. The Trump era's impact will be felt over decades to come, and a complete understanding of it is crucial. I now finish by discussing the reasons why this book was written.

Discussion

This book's research flowed from a theoretical paradigm in which attempts at persuasion through communication will often fail. However, my theory also allows that rhetoric can be influential in specific subsets of the population under exacting conditions that are optimal for influence to occur. The intensity of Trump's rhetoric, combined with the lack of long-term political socialization by second-generation Americans, created an environment where persuasion through communication occurs. Under most situations, the extant conditions would work against rhetoric being influential.

I undertook this research to encourage policymakers to look beyond the easy generalizations commonly made about public opinion about immigration and to instead use empirical evidence to make better decisions. How to incorporate immigrant populations is a crucial issue for advanced industrial nations (Putnam 2007). Gaining knowledge about the impact of elite rhetoric toward incorporation may allow insights that facilitate better immigration policies. Policymakers may create positive intergroup relations in an era of increased anti-immigration feelings, which would have a long-term beneficial impact. The increasing foreign-born population presents several opportunities for civil society. This knowledge can result in educational programs that allow for better policies. Immigration potentially offers excellent advantages for the United States (Smith and Edmonston 1997). Increasing the supply of high- and low-skill workers will benefit the economy significantly as the birthrate declines (United Nations Population Division 2000).

Determining the impact of rhetoric toward incorporation will guide how to provide an environment conducive to successfully incorporating new immigrants. For example, if encounters with immigrants reduce negative beliefs, then policymakers and activists can sponsor networking opportunities with immigrants to improve intergroup relations. I researched this book with these goals in mind, and I hope that future researchers will continue along this path to foster greater incorporation.

References

Adler, Leonore Loeb, and Uwe Peter Gielen. 2001. *Cross-Cultural Topics in Psychology*. 2nd ed. Westport, CT: Praeger.

Appiah, Kwame Anthony. 2005. *The Ethics of Identity*. Princeton: Princeton University Press.

Bourhis, Richard Y., Lena Celine Moise, Stephane Perreault, and Sacha Senecal.

1997. "Towards an Interactive Acculturation Model: A Social Psychological Approach." *International Journal of Psychology* 32 (6): 369–86.
Brislin, Richard W. 2000. *Understanding Culture's Influence on Behavior*. 2nd ed. Belmont, CA: Wadsworth.
Brubaker, Rogers. 2001. "The Return of Assimilation? Changing Perspectives on Immigration and Its Sequels in France, Germany, and the United States." *Ethnic and Racial Studies* 24 (4): 531–48.
Camicia, Steve P., and Cinthya M. Saavedra. 2009. "A New Childhood Social Studies Curriculum for a New Generation of Citizenship." *International Journal of Children's Rights* 17 (3): 501–17.
Campbell, Bradley, and Jason Manning. 2014. "Microaggression and Moral Cultures." *Comparative Sociology* 13 (6): 692–726.
Chryssochoou, Xenia. 2003. *Cultural Diversity: Its Social Psychology*. London: Blackwell.
Dale, Peter N. 1986. *The Myth of Japanese Uniqueness*. London: Routledge.
Deaux, Kay. 2011. "An Immigrant Frame for American Identity." *Applied Developmental Science* 15 (2): 70–72.
Downs, Donald A. 2012. "Civic Education versus Civic Engagement." *Academic Questions* 25 (3): 343–47.
Furco, Andrew, and Susan Root. 2010. "Research Demonstrates the Value of Service Learning." *Phi Delta Kappan* 91 (5): 16–20.
Goldstein, Susan Meyer. 2000. *Cross-Cultural Explorations: Activities in Culture and Psychology*. Needham Heights, MA: Allyn and Bacon.
Hollinger, David A. 2006. *Postethnic America: Beyond Multiculturalism*. New York: Basic Books.
Huntington, Samuel P. 2004. *Who Are We? The Challenges to America's National Identity*. New York: Simon and Schuster.
Kateb, George. 2006. *Patriotism and Other Mistakes*. New Haven: Yale University Press.
Kim, Thomas P. 2007. *The Racial Logic of Politics: Asian Americans and Party Competition*. Philadelphia: Temple University Press.
Kuo, Alexander, Neil Malhotra, and Cecilia Hyunjung Mo. 2014. "Why Do Asian Americans Identify as Democrats? Testing Theories of Social Exclusion and Intergroup Commonality." Research Paper No.1-2014. Nashville, TN: Vanderbilt Center for the Study of Democratic Institutions.
MacIntyre, Alasdair. 1995. "Is Patriotism a Virtue?" In *Theorizing Citizenship*, edited by Ronald Beiner, 209–28. Albany: State University of New York Press.
McCabe, Janice. 2009. "Racial and Gender Microaggressions on a Predominantly White Campus: Experiences of Black, Latina/o, and White Undergraduates." *Race, Gender and Class* 16 (1–2): 133–51.
Nussbaum, Martha C. 2012. "Teaching Patriotism: Love and Critical Freedom." *University of Chicago Law Review* 79:215–51.
Osanloo, Azadeh F. 2011. "Unburying Patriotism: Critical Lessons in Civics and Leadership Ten Years Later." *High School Journal* 95 (1): 56–71.
Pompa, Lori. 2002. "Service-Learning as Crucible: Reflections on Immersion, Context, Power, and Transformation." *Michigan Journal of Community Service Learning* 9 (3): 67–76.

Pratto, Felicia, and Anthony F. Lemieux. 2001. "The Psychological Ambiguity of Immigration and Its Implications for Promoting Immigration Policy." *Journal of Social Issues* 57 (3): 413–30.

Putnam, Robert D. 2000. *Bowling Alone: The Collapse and Revival of American Community.* New York: Simon and Schuster.

Putnam, Robert D. 2007. "Diversity and Community in the Twenty-First Century: The 2006 Johan Skytte Prize Lecture." *Scandinavian Political Studies* 30 (2): 137–74.

Richey, Sean E. 2010. "The Impact of Anti-Assimilationist Beliefs on Attitudes Towards Immigration." *International Studies Quarterly* 54 (1): 197–212.

Shiraev, Eric B., and David A. Levy. 2007. *Cross-Cultural Psychology: Critical Thinking and Contemporary Applications.* 3rd ed. Boston: Allyn and Bacon.

Smith, James P., and Barry Edmonston, eds. 1997. *The New Americans: Economic, Demographic, and Fiscal Effects of Immigration.* Washington, DC: National Academy Press.

Smith, Peter B., Michael Harris Bond, and Çigdem Kâgitçibasi. 2006. *Understanding Social Psychology across Cultures: Living and Working in a Changing World.* London: Sage.

Spencer, Margaret Beale. 2011. "American Identity: Impact of Youths' Differential Experiences in Society on Their Attachment to American Ideals." *Applied Developmental Science* 15 (2): 61–69.

United Nations Population Division. 2000. "Replacement Migration: Is It a Solution to Declining and Ageing Populations?" New York: United Nations.

Wing Sue, Derald, Christina M. Capodilupo, Gina C. Torino, Jennifer M. Bucceri, Aisha M. B. Holder, Kevin L. Nadal, and Marta Esquilin. 2007. "Racial Microaggressions in Everyday Life: Implications for Clinical Practice." *American Psychologist* 62 (4): 271–86.

Yamagishi, Toshio. 2003. "Trust and Social Intelligence in Japan." In *The State of Civil Society in Japan*, edited by Frank J. Schwartz and Susan J. Pharr, 281–87. Cambridge: Cambridge University Press.

Yamagishi, Toshio, and Midori Yamagishi. 1994. "Trust and Commitment in the United States and Japan." *Motivation and Emotion* 18 (2): 129–65.

Appendix

TABLE A1. Test of Unit Homogeneity

Female	0.03	(0.46)
Age	−0.04	(0.33)
Income	0.03	(0.49)
Education	−0.03	(0.50)
Asian	0.03	(0.44)
Black	0.02	(0.10)
Hispanic	−0.04	(0.33)
Ideology	−0.01	(0.75)

TABLE A2. Effect of Treatment Conditions

Variable	Patriotism	(S.E.)	American Identity	(S.E.)
Trump-Immigration	−0.526*	0.215	−0.447*	0.209
Trump-Trade	0.141	0.224	−0.082	0.219
Cut point 1	−3.416***	0.280	−4.089***	0.360
Cut point 2	−1.875***	0.183	−2.800***	0.225
Cut point 3	−0.109	0.154	−1.446***	0.167
Cut point 4			0.060	0.151
N	451		451	
χ^2	10.219**		5.128	

TABLE A3. Survey Questionnaire

- Q1 Are you a US citizen? Yes (1) No (2) If No Is Selected, Then Skip to End of Block
- Q2 Where were your parents born? Both were born in the United states (1) One was born in the United States and one outside the United States. (2) Both were born outside the United States (3) If Both were born in the Unite . . . Is Selected, Then Skip to End of Block
- Q3 Are you male or female? Male (1) Female (2)
- Q4 What is your current age? (U.S. Census) 18 to 19 (1) 20 to 24 (2) 25 to 34 (3) 35 to 44 (4) 45 to 54 (5) 55 to 64 (6) 65 or over (7)
- Q5 What is your combined annual household income? Less than 30,000 (1) 30,000–39,999 (2) 40,000–49,999 (3) 50,000–59,999 (4) 60,000–69,999 (5) 70,000–79,999 (6) 80,000–89,999 (7) 90,000–99,999 (8) 100,000 or more (9)
- Q6 What is your race? White (1) Black or African American (2) Asian or Pacific Islander (3) Native American (4) Other (5) Multiracial (6)
- Q7 Are you Hispanic or Latino? Yes (1) No (2)
- Q8 If you are Hispanic or Latino, what area does your ancestry come from? Mexico (1) Cuba (2) Puerto Rico (3) Central America (4) South America (5) Dominican Republic (6) Some other place (7)
- Q9 What is the highest level of education you have completed? Less than High School (1) High School / GED (2) Some College (3) 4-year College Degree (4) Masters Degree (5) Doctoral Degree (6)
- Q10 What political party do you typically support? Democratic (1) Republican (2) Not any party (3) Some other party (4)
- Q11 What best describes your political ideology? Very Conservative (1) Somewhat Conservative (2) A Little Conservative (3) Neither Conservative or Liberal
- (4) A Little Liberal (5) Somewhat Liberal (6) Very Liberal (7)
- Q31 Donald Trump is the leading candidate for the Republican Party's nomination for President. He opposes illegal immigration, and wants to build a wall to keep out those coming in illegally from Mexico. He says that illegal immigrants commit crimes and take jobs away from Americans.
- Q32 According to the passage that you just read, Donald Trump says illegal immigrants do what? Commit crimes, Get welfare, I did not read it carefully (6)
- Q33 What do you think of Donald Trump's ideas on immigration? I fully agree with his ideas, I somewhat agree with his ideas, I somewhat disagree with his ideas, I fully disagree with his ideas (7)
- Q34 Donald Trump is the leading candidate for the Republican Party's nomination for President. He is opposed to current international free trade deals, and wants to scrap these deals or renegotiate them. He says that the countries in these deals commit currency manipulation against the United States dollar and take jobs away from Americans.

    According to the passage that you just read, Donald Trump says countries in these free trade deals do what to the United States? Manipulate currency, Abuse human rights, I did not read it carefully (6)
- Q36 What do you think of Donald Trump's ideas on international free trade deals? I fully agree with his ideas (4), I somewhat agree with his ideas (5), I somewhat disagree with his ideas, I fully disagree with his ideas (7)
- Q37 "Birdwatching, or birding, is a form of wildlife observation in which the observation of birds is a recreational activity. It can be done with the naked eye, through a visual enhancement device like binoculars and telescopes, or by listening for bird sounds. This hobby has become very popular recently." From Wikipedia

- Q38 According to the passage that you just read, birdwatching has recently become? Less popular (10) Very popular, I did not read it carefully (6)
- Q39 What do you think of birdwatching's popularity?
  - ☐ I fully agree with it (4)
  - ☐ I somewhat agree with it (5)
  - ☐ I somewhat disagree with it (6)
  - ☐ I fully disagree with it (7)
- Q52 About how often do experiences of discrimination based on your race or ethnicity happen to you personally in the United States?
  - ☐ Less than Once a Month (4)
  - ☐ Once a Month (5)
  - ☐ 2–3 Times a Month (6)
  - ☐ Once a Week (7)
  - ☐ 2–3 Times a Week (8)
  - ☐ Daily (9)
- Q49 Now speaking of immigration, which of the two options below do you think it is best for the children of immigrants to do:
  - ☐ Maintain the distinct culture of their parents' home country and not to try to fit into American culture. (4)
  - ☐ Try to fit into American culture and not maintain the distinct culture of their parents' home country. (5)
- Q47 Who do you support in the 2016 Presidential Race?
  - ☐ Hillary Clinton (4)
  - ☐ Bernie Sanders (5)
  - ☐ Donald Trump (6)
  - ☐ Marco Rubio (7)
  - ☐ Ted Cruz (8)
  - ☐ John Kasich (9)
  - ☐ Some other candidate. (10)
  - ☐ I have not decided yet.
- Q48 What political party do you typically support? Democratic, Republican, Not any party, Some other party
- Q50 How do you feel about the United States of America?, Hate it (4), Dislike it (5), Neither like nor dislike it, Like it, Love it (8)
- Q51 How important is being an American to you personally? Extremely important (4) Very important (5) Somewhat important (6), A little important (7), Not at all important (8)

TABLE A4. Summary Statistics

Variable	Mean	Std. Dev.	Min.	Max.	N
Unpatriotic	1.431	0.691	1	5	5,564
Validated voter	0.683	0.465	0	1	1,656
Conspiracy theories	0	1.252	−2.172	4.41	4,858
Birtherism	1.769	0.930	1	4	5,349
Obamacare death panels	2.175	0.993	1	4	5,048
Truthism	2.27	0.924	1	4	5,441
Katrina flooding	1.757	0.808	1	4	5,398
Future economy	0.137	0.343	0	1	5,845
Political trust	2.211	0.542	1	4	5,944
Efficacy	3.765	1.223	1	5	5,544
Dissatisfied with democracy	2.253	0.759	1	4	5,514
Muslims	45.184	23.374	0	100	5,463
Gays and lesbians	52.206	27.53	0	100	5,514
Immigration	2.542	1.075	1	5	5,453
Political knowledge	5.225	2.569	0	10	5,984
Media attention	10.398	4.055	0	23	5,984
Interest	3.368	1.118	1	5	5,981
Party ID	3.521	2.11	1	7	5,960
Age	7.424	3.331	1	13	5,923
Education	2.976	1.159	1	5	5,934
Hispanic	0.171	0.376	0	1	5,965
Black	0.192	0.394	0	1	5,984
Income	13.655	8.149	1	28	5,456
Female	0.519	0.5	0	1	5,984
Parents born abroad	1.344	0.708	1	3	5,967

TABLE A5. Correlation with Unpatriotic and Dependent Variables

	Unpatriotic	
Conspiracy theories	0.11	(0.00)
Birtherism	0.00	(0.99)
Trutherism	0.11	(0.00)
Obamacare death panels	0.02	(0.13)
Katrina flooding	0.16	(0.00)
Validated voter	−0.09	(0.00)
Future economy	0.00	(0.86)
Political trust	−0.07	(0.01)
Efficacy	−0.08	(0.00)
Dissatisfaction with democracy	0.16	(0.00)
Muslims	−0.02	(0.50)
Gays and lesbians	−0.03	(0.21)
Immigration	0.01	(0.62)

Note: p-values in parentheses.

Index

Note: References in *italic* and **bold** refer to figures and tables. References followed by "n" refer to footnotes.

agenda-setting mechanism, 73
American identity, 2, 4, 9, 12, 25, 49, 72, 87–90, 138; dependent variables, 80–81; determinants of, **88**; histogram of, 83, *85*; in incorporation, 75–77; treatment effects, *84, 85*
American National Election Study (ANES) survey, 42–44; external validity, 87–88; non-second-generation Americans, *44*; Republican Party rhetoric, 109–14; second-generation Americans, *43, 44*
amplification, 140
anti-immigration feelings, 5, 39, 41, 148
anti-immigration rhetoric, 12, 71–90; cues of identity, 74–75; dependent variables, 80–81; elite academic literature, 73–74; ethnicity of participant, 83–84, 87; experimental procedures, 78–79; external validity with ANES survey data, 87–88; heuristics, 73–74; histogram of exposure, 82, *83, 85*; illegal immigrants, 71; incorporation levels, 76–78; manipulation check, 81; patriotism, 75–76, 80, *83*, 87–88, **88**; predictions, 78; stimuli, 79–80, *82*; on subgroups, 27–28; Trump and, 12–13, 93–115. *See also* political communication
anti-incorporation pressures, 140–41
Asian Americans: ANES survey, 125; COVID-19 pandemic, 140; datasets, 13, 118; impression of Trump, *127*; linked fate with immigrants, 99; NAAS Post-Election study, 124; ordered probit regression models, **86**; pairwise correlation, 126; pan-ethnic groupings, 74, 117; Republican party identification of, **106**, 128–29, *129*; second-generation, 124–29; voting for Trump, *128*
assimilationism, 146

Bangladeshi Americans, 126
base-mobilization strategies, 94
Buchanan, Patrick, 10
Bush, Jeb, 68

Cambodian Americans, 126
Carson, Ben, 67
Castro, Fidel, 117

children of immigrants, 1, 18, 36, 76, 88, 96, 109; ANES survey, 77; anti-immigrantion statements, 58; attuned to anti-immigration rhetoric, 11, 35; census data, 72; civic engagement of, 138; explicit parental support, 49; incorporation process of, 2; national-level rhetoric, 115; protest movements, 5; survey methodology, 54; on undocumented immigrants, 74. *See also* second-generation Americans
Chinese Americans, 126, 127
Cho, Tam, 2
Clinton, Hillary, 73
cognitive dissonance, 133
collateral damage, 9; changeable attitudes (lemma 3), 48–51; conditions necessary for, 11–12, 35–55; definition of, 11; establishing Trump's rhetoric (lemma 1), 36–41; lack of intent, 2016 Trump's rhetoric (lemma 4), 51–54; political communication, 2–3, 18–31; second-generation Americans (lemma 2), 42–48
collateral damage theory, 11, 18–31; anti-immigration rhetoric on subgroups, 27–28; communication, 29–30; conditional effects, 22–25; minimal effects paradigm, 19–22; second-generation Americans, 29–30; theoretical expectations, 27–28
community of culture, 50
community of interests, 50
conditional effects, 22–25; Rescorla-Wagner model, 25; Shannon and Weaver model, 23; Stimulus-Organism-Response (S-O-R) model, 23–25
confounding, 79
conservative second-generation Americans: exposure effects, **109**; Republican Party rhetoric, 104, *104*; Trump approval, *108*, 108–9, **109**

Cotton, Tom, 9
Cuban Americans: national ancestral origins, 74; political socialization, 28; Republican Party identification, 6, 13, 28, 118, 133–34; Salvadoran Americans *vs.*, 117; second-generation, 120, *123*, 124; single-issue voters, 117–18; Trump presidency, 14, 120
cue taking, 73–74

Democratic Party, 6, 6n4, 46, 51, 53, 110, 120, 132–33
dependent variables, 80–81
Dewey, John, 19
differentialist turn, 140
disaggregation, second-generation Americans, 13–14, 117–34
Dominican Americans, 117, 119–20

elite rhetoric literature, 73–74; agenda-setting mechanism, 73; cue taking, 73–74
Emerson, Rupert, 35n1
experimental stimuli, *82, 83*

Franklin, Benjamin, 57

Goldwater, Barry, 117
group-based affinity, 50

heuristics, 73–74
Hispanic Americans, 142; ANES, 77; assimilation of, 83; ordered probit regression models, **86**; pan-ethnic groupings, 74, 117; Republican Party identification, **105**; second-generation Americans, 114
histogram, 82, *83, 85*
hypodermic needle effect, 20

illegal immigrants, 3, 71; non-second-generation Americans, *44*; second-generation Americans, *44*; thermometer ratings, *44*, **45**

immigrant-bashing, 36
immigrant identity, 50
immigration incorporation: academic debates, 4–7; current levels, 76–78; future of, 136–38; measures of, 138; Trump and, 18, 36
immigration tweets, **60**, 63, **63**, 65

Japanese Americans, 125–28

Kate's Law, 61
King, Steve, 9, 38, 102
Kobach, Kris, 9
Korean Americans, 74, 87, 117, 126, 128

labeling theory, 75
Latino Americans, 119–24; ANES question, 123; build the wall, 122–23; dichotomous question, 123; opinions on changes, 120, *121*, *122*; Pew study, 119–20
LexisNexis, 37, 40
linked fate with immigrants, 96–99
Lippmann, Walter, 19

manipulation check, 81
mass media, 10, 19–21, 31
McCain, John, 38
medium effects, 23
Mexican Americans, 119–24, 133; attenuated impact for, 119; build-the-wall, 13, *125*; dislike of Trump, 121, *124*; national ancestral origin, 74; second-generation, 13, 27, 118, 120–24, *124*; targeted samples, 118; voting for Trump, 120, *123*
microaggressions, 141–42
minimal effects paradigm, 19–22
mobilization, 6, 27, 94
multinomial logit model, 109
multinomial probit regression model, 107

National Academies of Sciences, 77
National Asian American Survey, 119
non-second-generation Americans, 28, 48, 132; agreement levels with Trump's ideas, 97; agreement with respondent, *98*; illegal immigrants, *44*; intermarriage, 137; linked fate with immigrants, 96–98; Trump's immigration ideas, 96; undocumented immigrants, 35

Obama, Barack, 62, 67
ordered logistic regression models, *85*, 113
ordered probit regression models: for Asian Americans, **86**; for Hispanic Americans, **86**

Pakistani Americans, 127, 134
partisan estrangement, 94–96
partisan identification, 93
partisan recruitment, 94–96
patriotism, 71n1, 80; ANES measures, 87–88; determinants of, **88**; histogram of exposure, *83*; in incorporation, 75–76
perceived discrimination, 74
Pérez, Efrén O., 29
political communication, 1–2, 4; academic debates, 8; collateral damage theory, 18–31; conditional effects, 22–25; minimal effects paradigm, 19–22. *See also* anti-immigration rhetoric
political socialization, 11, 18, 25, 35, 48, 50–51, 89, 93, 136–37
probit regression model, 102
public opinion toward immigrations, 10n5

quantitative text analysis, 62–64

randomization, 72
Reagan, Ronald, 13, 28, 117
receiver effects, 23
reforming incorporation, 143–44
refugees, 142

Republican Party rhetoric, 12–13, 93–115; ANES survey data, 109–14; conservative second-generation Americans, 104, *104*, 108–9; ethnicity of participants, 104–5; experimental procedures, 100–101; experimental results, 102; factors, 94; linked fate with immigrants, 96–99; partisan estrangement, 94–96; partisan identification, 93; predictions, 99–100; Presidential Vote model, 110, **111**; results replication, 109–14; second-generation Americans, 102, 105, 107; stimuli, 100–101; Trump approval, 105, *106*, **107**, 107–9, *108*, **109**; voting determinants, **112**, **113**

Republican Presidential nominees, 46–48, *47*, *48*

Rescorla-Wagner model, 25

research topics: anti-immigration rhetoric, 144–46; anti-incorporation pressures, 140–41; lack of intention, 141–42; microaggressions, 141–42; reforming incorporation, 143–44; refugees, 142; social trust, 143; Trump's impact on supporters, 139–40

rhetorical analysis, 12, 57–69; list of campaigns, 59, 61–62; overview of, 57–58; presidential speeches mentioning immigration/immigrants, 65–66, **66**; sentiment analysis, 62–66, **63**; specific examples, 58–62; Trump's anti-immigration rhetoric, 66–68; Trump's immigration tweets, 63, **63**, 65

Romney, Mitt, 38

Rove, Karl, 94

Rubio, Marco, 68

Salvadoran Americans, 117, 118, 119–21

second-generation Americans: ANES survey, *43*, *44*; collateral damage theory, 29–30; communication, 29–30; disaggregating, 13–14, 117–34; ethnic subgroups of, 13; governmental trust, *95*; intermarriage, 137; lack of socialization, 26; level of integration, 29; Republican Party identification, 102; Republican Presidential nominees, 46–48, *47*, *48*; Trump approval, 105, *106*, 107; Trump's rhetoric, 2016 (lemma 2), 42–48; voting determinants, **113**. *See also* children of immigrants

second-generation Americans attitudes, 13–14, 117–34; Asian Americans, 124–29; building the wall, 122–24, *125*, 130, *131*; Latinos, 119–24; party identification, 131–33; political geography, 129–31; voting, 131–33, **132**

segmented assimilation, 4–5

sender effects, 23

Sender-Message-Channel-Receiver model, 23

Shannon, Claude Elwood, 23

Shannon and Weaver model, 23

social desirability bias, 97

social identity theory, 75

social trust, 143

sociological labeling theory, 75

Spanish Americans, 119–20

Steinle, Kate, 61

stigmatization, 75

stimuli, 79–80, *82*

Stimulus-Organism-Response (S-O-R) model, 23–25

supporters, Trump's impact, 139–40

Tancredo, Tom, 10, 102

Trump, Donald, 2, 7, 12–13, 21, 55, 76, 118, 134; anti-immigration rhetoric, 12–13, 35, 66–68; ballot variable, 110; establishing Trump's rhetoric, 36–41; immigration tweets, **60**, **63**, 65; lack of intent, 2016 Trump's rhetoric, 51–54; polling support, *68*; presidential speeches mentioning immigration/immigrants, 65–66, **66**; rhetorical analysis, 12, 57–69; second-generation Americans and, 42–48

two-tiered pluralism, 94

undocumented immigrants, 59, 74, 78

Vietnamese Americans: communism, 118; national ancestral origins, 74; political socialization, 28; Republican Party identification, 6, 13, 28, 118, 133–34; Trump presidency, 14

word-presence technique, 64